STEPHEN JEFFREYS

is best known for his property comedy *Valued Friends*, which enjoyed two sell-out runs at Hampstead Theatre in 1989 and 1990 and won him the *Evening Standard* award for the Most Promising Playwright.

He was discovered at the 1977 National Student Drama Festival, where *Like Dolls or Angels*, a study of a stuntman on the skids, won the *Sunday Times* Playwriting Award. Stephen then helped to set up the touring company Pocket Theatre Cumbria, for whom he wrote a number of plays including an adaptation of *Hard Times* (1982) which has been performed all over the world. His Spanish Civil War version of *Carmen* for Communicado won an Edinburgh Fringe First and was performed at the Tricycle Theatre in 1985.

Most recently he has written *The Clink* (1990) for Paines Plough (Riverside Studios) and adapted *A Jovial Crew* for the RSC (Swan 1992, Barbican Pit 1993). Stephen is Literary Associate for the Royal Court Theatre, and is currently writing a film, *A Neutral State*, with Max Stafford-Clark.

D1341572

Other Volumes in this Series

STEPHEN JEFFREYS

A GOING CONCERN

NICK HERN BOOKS
London

To my mother

A Nick Hern Book

A Going Concern first published in Great Britain 1993
as a paperback original by Nick Hern Books Limited,
14 Larden Road, London W3 7ST
A Going Concern copyright © 1993 by Stephen Jeffreys

Typeset by Country Setting, Woodchurch, Kent TN26 3TB
Printed by Cox & Wyman Ltd, Reading, Berks

A CIP catalogue record for this book is available from
the British Library

ISBN 1-85459-270-X

Characters

JOHN CHAPEL	(called Chapel)	seventy-five
JACK	Chapel's son	fifty
GORDON	Chapel's son	late forties
DAVID	Jack's son	twenty
TONY	Gordon's son	twenty-six
BARRY	Jack and Gordon's nephew	twenty-three
RAY		around thirty
VICKY		early twenties

The action of the play takes place in the larger workshop of Chapel and Sons (Billiards) Ltd. in the City Road, London.

ACT ONE takes place one Friday in April 1966.
ACT TWO takes place the following Friday.

The workshop is an oblong room with a wooden floor. Frosted windows run the length of the upstage wall. A sink with an Ascot and a tiled draining board is up left. To the right of the draining board is a gas fire and a gas hob with kettle and billiard irons in its vicinity.

To the right of that, a workbench (TONY's) cluttered with clock mechanisms. Against the stage right wall is another bench (BARRY's). On a shelf above the bench is a large valve radio and a filthy copy of the 1901 Factory Act. Downstage left is an area full of boxes of old billiard balls and newly painted skittles.

Every cranny of the room is filled with junk associated with the business – the accumulation of over seventy years. A swing door right, leads off to a store area which leads to Jack's office and the front door. A doorway left leads into the other workshop and the side door which gives onto a parking area. At the start of the play, two bar billiard table bases and two tops (separate on trestles) fill the space. A third top is propped up against a wall.

The front door activates a shop warning bell when opened.
The telephone in Jack's office is wired to a bell which rings in the workshop.

A Going Concern was first staged at Hampstead Theatre, London, on 2 September 1993 with the following cast:

CHAPEL	Henry Stamper
JACK	David Horovitch
GORDON	David Killick
DAVID	Adam Godley
TONY	Reece Dinsdale
BARRY	James Clyde
RAY	Shaun Prendergast
VICKY	Samantha Holland

Directed by Matthew Lloyd
Designed by Sue Plummer
Lighting design by Leonard Tucker
Artistic Director Jenny Topper

ACT ONE, Scene One

Zoot Money and the Big Roll Band: 'Big Time Operator'. Lights come up slowly on the main workshop of Chapel Bros. It's around 9.30 a.m. The kettle is heating on the gas hob. DAVID is sweeping the floor. BARRY is at his bench, tacking a strip of cloth to a cushion. GORDON stands over him. Music fades.

GORDON. The Sun in Splendour.

BARRY. What about the Sun in Splendour?

GORDON. On the telephone yesterday. Ring any bells?

BARRY. Yesterday? The Sun in Splendour?

GORDON. Yes.

BARRY. It wasn't the Sun in Splendour, it was the Bricklayer's Arms.

GORDON. It was the Sun in Splendour.

BARRY. It wasn't the Sun –

GORDON. The Bricklayer's Arms? You mean the Bricklayer's Arms in the City?

BARRY. The Bricklayer's Arms, Dalston.

GORDON. Dalston? There is no such pub.

BARRY. It's written down in the gone wrong book.

GORDON. Well if it's written down in the gone wrong book, we'll all be able to read it, won't we, a pub that doesn't exist. I'm talking about the Sun in Splendour, Portobello Road.

BARRY. It wasn't –

GORDON. The Landlord's just been on the phone. That's how I know. We should have been over there yesterday. Some crafty bastard's had the top up and tinkered with the clock. They're getting an extra fifteen minutesworth for their sixpence, we've been losing money on the site for the last twenty-four hours.

BARRY. Well they didn't phone –

GORDON. The landlord phoned yesterday –

BARRY. They did not phone.

GORDON. David will you please fetch me the gone wrong book
please.

DAVID *goes off right.*

BARRY. The –

GORDON. Yes?

BARRY. The Bricklayer's Arms rang about something.

GORDON. Not the Bricklayer's Arms, Dalston, because there is
no such public house as the Bricklayer's Arms, Dalston.

BARRY. The other one then –

GORDON. The Bricklayer's Arms in the City –

BARRY. Wherever it is –

GORDON. It's in the City.

DAVID *is back with a large hard-covered notebook.*

GORDON. Thank you, David. Now then. Yesterday afternoon,
Thursday the fourteenth of April. The Sun in Splendour,
Portobello Road. Interference with clock. Playing time too
long. This is your handwriting, yes?

GORDON *holds the book out.* BARRY *turns away.*

I could have done it last night, if someone had had the wit to
tell me. I was in Shepherd's Bush. Tonight I'm in Rotherhithe,
very convenient, that's my weekend knackered before it's
begun.

He slams the book on a table top and steams out left. DAVID
sweeps. BARRY *hammers tacks into the cushion.*

BARRY. It definitely was.

DAVID. Yes.

BARRY. It was, I remember.

DAVID. I remember you saying. Dalston.

BARRY. David, don't sweep like that.

DAVID. Like what?

BARRY. You're raising too much dust. It all goes in my eyes.
Throw some water down first.

DAVID. I have.

BARRY. You need more.

DAVID *goes to the sink, fills a mug with water and with a
scooping motion, spreads it on the floor.*

BARRY. The whole point of having a gone wrong book is that people read it.

DAVID. Yes.

BARRY. We don't have a gone wrong conference period –

DAVID. What record you getting today?

BARRY. What?

DAVID. It's Friday, what record are you getting?

BARRY. How do you know I'm getting a record?

DAVID. This is my third Friday here. The first Friday you bought Sound of '65 by the Graham Bond Organisation. Last week it was Sonny Boy Williamson. These are the only two things I've ever seen you buy. So I deduced that every Friday you spend all your week's savings on a record.

BARRY. I should have said that to him. 'We have a gone wrong book, not a gone wrong conference period.'

DAVID *throws water on another part of the floor.*

DAVID. So what will it be?

BARRY. Actually, David, I never see you spending money either.

DAVID. Students don't have money, Barry, they have grants.

BARRY. I'd love to get out to the Sun in Splendour. He should think himself lucky. I'm stuck in this workshop. It strains your eyes and there's dust. I do the slog. Everyone else gets out. You'll get out this morning.

DAVID. Well, we'll swap over. You go out, I'll stay here.

BARRY. You can't do what I can do.

DAVID. I can cover cushions.

BARRY. It's not just cushions. Mending slates, cutting cloth, checking the ball channels.

DAVID. I thought you didn't like going out.

BARRY. It's out, isn't it?

JACK *comes in, right. He carries a letter.*

JACK. Gordon gone yet?

BARRY. No.

JACK. Man management. If I had no men to manage . . .

He wanders through towards the other workshop, then stops and turns back to DAVID.

Are you coming straight home tonight?

DAVID. No. I'm going to see a film.

JACK. Only your mother will want to–

DAVID. She knows.

JACK. Good, good. The management of men, the management of women . . .

> GORDON *is back.*

GORDON. Jack, I'm going to have to change my route. I've got to get out to the Portobello Road and no one else–

JACK. Have a look at this.

> JACK *shows him the letter.* GORDON *whips out glasses from a top pocket.* DAVID *has finished sweeping and now starts making the tea, collecting and washing mugs.*

What film you seeing?

DAVID. It's a Hungarian thing.

JACK. Oh. You know I've never met a Hungarian. Not one. The rest yes. The Hungarians no.

GORDON. Monday morning!

JACK. That's what it says.

GORDON. For the full-size.

JACK. For the full-size.

GORDON. The full-size won't be finished for Monday morning.

JACK. That's what I was checking with you.

GORDON. Monday *afternoon* the full size'll be finished.

JACK. Well the Old Man's booked the van for Monday morning.

GORDON. This is the icing on the cake, this is.

JACK. Did he tell you he was booking the van?

GORDON. He doesn't tell me anything, Jack.

JACK. I'll ring them up and cancel it.

GORDON. Monday afternoon it'll be ready.

JACK. I'll ring them up.

GORDON. Every bastard day something. He shouldn't be booking vans. He shouldn't be allowed within two furlongs of a telephone. He's seventy-five years old, he should be watching the two thirty at Chepstow on the telly.

JACK. It keeps him off the streets —

GORDON. We're running a business not a playground for the elderly. When Len died he got it into his head he was running the show again. Well he can't run the show, he's had his whole life and all he's proved is he knows the way to the City Arms and back. This cannot go on —

JACK. Well it's easy to say —

GORDON. If he was doing nothing which is what he did for forty years I wouldn't mind. I can't humour this, Jack, it takes me a day a week to undo his damage.

JACK. Have a word with him, make him understand —

GORDON. You have a word with him, Jack. You're the eldest.

GORDON *picks up the gone wrong book and motors out right. JACK surveys the workshop, claps his hands.*

JACK. The ordering of vans, the management of fathers, eh Barry?

But BARRY *carries on tacking the cushion.* DAVID *gets a slim paperback out of his coat pocket and studies it.*

Where's Tony, not in yet?

BARRY. Not in yet.

JACK. What was it he had yesterday?

BARRY. Mmmm, it was a migraine actually.

JACK. You know I never heard the word migraine till I was forty-five. Now everyone has them all the time.

BARRY. Mmmm.

JACK. What about Ray?

BARRY. Not in yet.

JACK. Not in yet. Well we're very lucky to have an employee of the London fire brigade moonlighting for us. I suppose he can make up his own mind when he comes in.

BARRY. I suppose so.

JACK. You suppose so.

JACK *looks at* DAVID.

Revising?

DAVID. Yes.

JACK. Some aren't in yet, some have migraines, others are revising. What did Mr. Wilson call it, the white heat of the technological revolution?

DAVID. I'm making the tea.

JACK. Ah!

DAVID. I've swept the floor, now I'm making the tea. What are
you doing?

JACK. I was in at eight o'clock cooking the books. No men to
manage, no phone. It was like Butlin's.

*RAY comes in left. He is clothed from head to toe in black
leather biking gear and crash helmet. Throughout the
following, he removes the leathers and puts on a brown
workcoat over shirt and jeans.*

RAY. Don't expect anything out of me today, Jack. Fucking forty-
eight hours on, first forty quiet as the grave, not a shout, not a
dicky bird, nothing. We was playing volleyball all day. Got to
bed midnight. Half two, off goes the alarm. Down the pole,
heart pounding, fucking RTA job, Battle Bridge Road. This mini,
Tony wants to watch his self in his, pulled out in front of this
lorry, bang. Course, the filth have got there first haven't they,
they're giving it the works, mouth to mouth, radio the heart
crash team, all this, I says to the copper, forget it. Took us two
and a half hours to cut the geezer out, well dead. They're like
egg boxes them things, smash, well dead, dead on impact. Back
to the station, haven't had my head down five minutes, just
dropping off, another shout. Back in the wagon, storming down
the road, bell clanging away. Only a timber yard fire, isn't it,
not even on our patch, Newington Church Street, fucking eight
pump job, well alight, three hours at it, we finally get it under
control half past seven this morning. Haven't had time for a
shit, a shower, nothing. If I drop off today, don't even think of
waking me up, don't expect any work out of me whatever you
do, and don't for a moment get me to drive anywhere, lift
anything heavy or be nice to anyone, especially Gordon. Who's
got the Mirror, I need to look at the Cheltenham card before I
do anything else. Ta, David. Barry you look about as useful as a
pork chop in a synagogue. I'm off for that shit now, I'll be back
in ten minutes, David and when I come back I want a cup of
tea, a packet of Woodbine, a deck chair, a gross of mogadon
and a blow-job off that waitress in Mario's caff. See to it.

He goes off to the lavatory.

DAVID. Where am I going to get a deck chair from?

JACK. It's so decent of him to turn up at all. We only pay him
money.

*DAVID has made the tea. JACK goes to a wall cupboard and
gets out a small box of chalk and a red ball. Over the next few
minutes he parcels these neatly with brown paper and string.*

DAVID. Right, how many are we? Is the Old Man in?

JACK. The guv'nor? We won't see him this side of a large brandy and soda.

DAVID. Just six then.

> TONY *comes in. He carries something in a brown paper bag. He puts the bag down on his bench.*

JACK. Tony. Seven.

TONY (*quiet, not looking up*). Jack.

DAVID. Hi Tony.

JACK. Traffic bad?

TONY. The traffic was the traffic.

JACK. How's the migraine?

TONY. The migraine's gone. I had the migraine yesterday.

JACK. I was saying. I never heard the word migraine –

TONY. The migraine's gone, Jack.

> BARRY *has finished his cushion. He places the three assembled cushions on the table top and starts screwing them in.* TONY *watches him.*

BARRY. Which one of these is which?

TONY. Are you talking to me?

BARRY. There's two tables going out this morning, I don't know which should be which.

TONY. You are talking to me. There are two what?

BARRY. Two tables.

TONY. Two tables. And?

BARRY. One has to go to a pub in Tottenham, the other's a private buyer. Which is which?

TONY. How the fuck should I know?

BARRY. Well, Tony, you usually –

TONY. Was I here yesterday?

BARRY. No –

TONY. Did you *see* me yesterday?

BARRY. I thought –

TONY. Look at them.

BARRY. What?

TONY. Look at the tables. You spent all yesterday doing these tables up. You tell me.

BARRY. Well. This one here is . . . it's a good table it's got like . . . old-fashioned legs . . .

JACK. Like an old Wilder.

TONY. Like an old Wilder, that could be a clue, Barry.

BARRY. Whereas this one is a straightforward Snookerette–

TONY. So.

BARRY. So . . .

TONY. Where's the pub?

BARRY. Tottenham.

TONY. So what will the table look like after a couple of weeks in a pub in Tottenham?

BARRY. Like shit.

TONY. Shit, exactly. So who gets the old-fashioned legs?

BARRY. The private buyer.

TONY *claps* BARRY *round the shoulder*.

TONY. Executive brains.

TONY *turns towards* DAVID *who is pouring the tea*.

Tea ready, David?

DAVID. It's ready.

TONY. You got in, you swept the floor, you made the tea.

DAVID. In that order, how did you guess?

DAVID *goes to the door left and shouts*.

Tea, Arthur.

There's a general milling for tea. TONY, JACK *and* DAVID *take mugs. After a while* BARRY *collects his*.

TONY. What's the book, David?

DAVID. Revision.

TONY (*lunging*). Let's have a butcher's.

DAVID. No.

DAVID. Leave off.

TONY. Give us it.

TONY *gets the book from* DAVID'*s pocket.*

Minor poets of the nineteenth century.

DAVID. Give us it here.

TONY. Ernest Dowson. Eighteen sixty-seven to nineteen hundred. It's all in Latin.

DAVID. That's just the title.

TONY. Hmmm.

DAVID. Give us it back, Tony.

TONY. They are not long, the weeping and the laughter,
Love and desire and hate:
I think they have no portion in us after
We pass the gate.

GORDON *comes in. He stands, stopped in his tracks.*

They are not long, the days of wine and roses:
Out of a misty dream
Our path emerges for a while, then closes
Within a dream.

Pause.

JACK. Is that all?

DAVID. I think that's the point the poet's trying to make.

TONY *hands the book back to* DAVID.

TONY. The days of wine and roses.

GORDON. Some people seem to have an awful lot of time to stand around in this life. Right then, let's get moving, who's going where? Ray . . . Where's Ray?

TONY. Having a shit.

GORDON. Can't he do that in the fire brigade's time?

DAVID. Do you know the British labourer spends seven per cent of all working hours in the lavatory. It was in the Daily Express so it must be true.

GORDON. That's how that fat little Herbert from Huddersfield won the election, is it?

DAVID. Good platform. A vote for Wilson is a vote for the bog.

GORDON. Now who've we got? Ray, David, Tony . . . I've got to get out to the Mile End Road. And there's the Sun in Splendour. You're going that way aren't you Tony?

TONY. No.

GORDON. Where are you going then?

TONY. Cricklewood.

GORDON. Then you can do it on your way back.

TONY. From Cricklewood –

GORDON. Don't give me aggravation, someone made a mistake. It's a gone wrong, the clock's been interfered with, it's been buggered since the day before yesterday. These two tables are ready, David you go with Ray if you can put up with him.

DAVID. Fine.

GORDON. One of these is a private house. I suggest you take the better one down the pub, where is it?

BARRY. Tottenham.

GORDON. Yes, this is the better one, the Snookerette.

BARRY. No it isn't.

GORDON. I beg your pardon, Barry?

BARRY. This one here's better. Look at the legs.

GORDON. The legs? Who's going to look at the legs?

JACK. He's right, Barry, the Snookerette's better so take it down the pub.

JACK *winks at* TONY.

TONY. Executive brains, uncle.

JACK. Entrepreneurial brains.

RAY *enters, waving the Mirror. Picks up his tea.*

RAY. Breasley, a double, it came to me in a flash of divine revelation.

GORDON. We should start charging for that bog.

RAY. Hunter's Luck in the two thirty, Desperate Dan in the three fifteen. David, this tea tastes like Derv. I'm gonna get a roll from Mario's.

TONY. Mario's niece.

RAY. Is that his niece? She is a bit dainty, do admit.

DAVID. Take Arthur's tea through.

RAY *picks up the last mug of tea and goes left.*

TONY. Give her one from me.

RAY. Arthur, give it a rest, you're allowed tea breaks.

GORDON. Right. Another week over, good as. Get loaded.

People move to the sink as tea is drunk or thrown away.
DAVID *takes the van keys off a hook, picks up a cardboard box of accessories and goes left.*

TONY (*at his bench*). Where's the clock for Cricklewood? I left it here on Wednesday.

BARRY. Actually, Tony, it's on my bench.

TONY. What's it doing on your bench?

BARRY. I was just looking it over.

TONY. Looking it over, what is it, the Sporting Life?

BARRY. I was looking how you'd done it.

TONY. Oh great. This is great. Is it all right?

BARRY. It's fine.

TONY. You looked it over and it's fine, well that's fine, now can I have the fucking clock back, Barry?

BARRY *hands* TONY *the clock.* TONY *triggers the mechanism and watches it work.* DAVID *is back.*

DAVID. Van's open. Could someone help me with the –

BARRY. I'll do it.

BARRY *and* DAVID *go to either side of the table top nearest the door. They swivel the top so that its side is facing downwards and carry it out left.*

GORDON. Tony, if you could do the Sun in Splendour first–

TONY. I'm going to Cricklewood first –

GORDON. The Landlord's very upset –

TONY. I'm doing you a favour, Dad, I'll do it in my own time. Now. Clock. Keys.

GORDON. You'll need the A to Z.

TONY. Dad, I'll do the Sun in Splendour for you, I'll do Cricklewood. I have a customised mini, I have common sense. I don't need maps, or people checking my work, snow ploughs, anything. I get to the site, I do the job, I go to the next site, right? Right.

TONY *goes out left.*

GORDON. Tony!

JACK. Leave him.

GORDON. He can't talk to me like that.

JACK. He's the best of the bunch, give him his head.

GORDON. I'll give him his head. On a bleeding platter in the lunch hour.

JACK. The best of the bunch. Not that there's a fat lot of competition.

GORDON. You said it. How did Len have a son like Barry? Len could run the show on his own, Barry's mind is orbiting the earth in a sputnik.

JACK. He's still upset.

GORDON. He wasn't Einstein before it happened.

DAVID *and* BARRY *come back in. They go to the second table top and take it out.* JACK *addresses his parcel.*

GORDON. Is that for -?

JACK. Ipswich, yes.

GORDON. Good. Now the A.G.M. I got the papers from you. What about the accountant?

JACK. He's coming in this afternoon.

GORDON. Molyneux is?

JACK. Laurie Molyneux is coming in.

GORDON. And you know what you're doing.

JACK. Do I know what I'm doing? I sometimes wonder.

GORDON. Well Len always used to keep him on a tight rein so there was no poking around.

JACK. I'll look after Molyneux.

GORDON. Because those figures, what we give him, they're not completely on the level are they?

JACK. Nothing in this life is completely on the level.

GORDON. Just I thought there was a procedure. A gentleman's agreement. Len would take him out to lunch or something.

JACK. I'll look after Laurie Molyneux, Gordon.

GORDON. Just we keep coming across situations where Len and Len alone knew.

JACK. I'll look after the accountant.

GORDON. You still get people saying, 'How's your brother, he hasn't been in.'

JACK. We're doing fine.

DAVID and BARRY are back.

That private house, David, he'll have a cheque for you.

DAVID. I know.

They take the nearer of the bases and carry it out.

GORDON. We're not doing fine Jack. We're struggling. We're under the cosh and we keep pretending we aren't.

RAY is back with a can of coke and a ham roll.

RAY. It should not be allowed, there should be laws.

JACK. Actually, Ray, there *are* laws, she's under sixteen.

RAY. You ask her for a ham roll and she gives you two large mascaras and a hard-on.

GORDON. They're a Sicilian family, you'll wake up with your knackers set in concrete.

RAY is at the window, ogling the café.

RAY. Not a stitch on under that overall. She makes me come over all twitchy. Touch of the Ursula Andress.

JACK. The private house Ray, the bloke's got a cheque for you. Mr. Leitch, don't forget it.

RAY. I never forget anything. Are you sure she's under sixteen?

JACK. And he's a wealthy geezer, so ask him if he wants to buy the business and put us all out of our misery.

RAY. What can it be like? You wake up in the morning looking like that. Unreal. I wouldn't even get out of bed, I'd just lie there staring at meself.

DAVID and BARRY are back.

DAVID. Work, work, work, Ray, I never see you stop.

RAY. Have a night on the watch, David, then you'd know about work.

DAVID. Which cues do we take?

RAY. You can fuck off back to college.

DAVID. Can't wait.

JACK. I think we can run to a couple of good ones.

JACK delves among the cues in the corner.

BARRY. Just the last base to load, Ray.

RAY. I'm still eating my breakfast.

BARRY. Actually, I've got rather a lot to do today.

RAY. Well work faster.

JACK. These two. About as straight as you'll get.

RAY. Those two? Fucking hell, Jack, your old man's old man must have made those.

JACK. He probably likes antiques, he's bought one of our tables.

JACK *hands the cues to* DAVID. RAY *finishes his roll and coke, throwing the can and bag onto the floor.*

RAY. Right, who's coming with me?

BARRY. David.

RAY. Oh Jesus, I'll have to drive. I can't sleep properly when David's driving. Where's the keys?

DAVID *throws the keys fast at* RAY, *hoping he'll drop them, but* RAY *plucks them out of the air.*

RAY. Dig that. Colin Cowdrey.

DAVID. Come on then, twinkletoes.

DAVID *puts the cues and a case of tools into the last base. He and* RAY *carry it out.*

RAY. If we're not back by Tuesday we've been killed in action.

GORDON. So. You're doing what today, Barry?

BARRY. I'm doing the next table today. And on Monday I shall do the one after that.

GORDON. Good.

BARRY. Oh typical. They've forgotten the spirit level.

BARRY *picks up the spirit level and goes.* GORDON *rinses his mug at the tap.* JACK *makes to leave.*

JACK. One day they'll forget the table.

GORDON. Jack. We've got to face up to this one.

JACK *stops, but doesn't look at* GORDON.

He means well, we all mean well but that's not the point. We've been weak. The last six months, we've let him take over the reins again. Well he's not up to it. He's living in the nineteen thirties and that's on his good days. This is a family business but the business has to come before the family. If there's no business, you can't feed the family. He has to go. I can give him the bullet or you can give him the bullet.

JACK. No one can give him the bullet, he's the majority shareholder.

GORDON. He's the *largest* shareholder, Jack. If the rest of us stand together, you me and Barry, he has to go.

JACK. What are you saying, we take it to the A.G.M. and vote him out?

GORDON. That's the last resort –

JACK. It's his business, he made it what it is –

GORDON. In the last resort he has four hundred shares. I have two hundred, you have two hundred. Barry has Len's two hundred. It shouldn't come to it, but if it does, it'll be six hundred against four hundred.

Shouting and hooting outside as the van goes.

JACK. Does Barry agree with you?

GORDON. I don't know what Barry thinks.

JACK. Well, Barry might vote for the Old Man. That would be six hundred four hundred for him to stay–

GORDON. How should I know what Barry thinks? You'd need to be a brain surgeon with a very large crowbar to know what Barry thinks. Why don't you ask him?

JACK. Why don't *you* ask him, you're planning the takeover.

GORDON. I'm not planning a takeover –

JACK. That's what you're saying –

GORDON. How can I take over a business I'm already running–

JACK. It's a family business, we all run –

GORDON. I'm not crawling to Barry for his vote –

JACK. Well then we're stuck.

BARRY *comes in and goes over to his bench.*

GORDON. We're not stuck, Jack. You have to do one simple thing. It doesn't make any difference Barry coming back in, I don't care who hears. We have to take the bull by the horns on this one. I can give him the bullet or you can give him the bullet. But the bullet it will have to be. You're the eldest, it would be better coming from you.

JACK (*making to go*). Well –

GORDON. It's no good shrugging your shoulders and going off to hide in the office. We're in the front line out here.

BARRY. He's right. Do it.

Pause. GORDON and JACK are amazed.

GORDON. There you have it. In a nutshell. From the new shareholder.

JACK. All right.

GORDON. You'll tell the old man he's got to go.

Pause.

JACK. Yes.

GORDON. And you'll tell him today.

JACK. Why does it have to be today?

GORDON. Because the A.G.M. is next Friday. If we collar him today, there's time to put it on the agenda so it's there in black and white. He can have a week getting used to the idea and announce his retirement in front of the accountant. Then it'll be in the minutes and no one can say afterwards that it didn't happen.

Pause.

JACK. I'll tell him then. Today.

GORDON looks at JACK, then turns and goes left.

The management of men . . . the management of fathers . . . Barry, what do you do when you're not here? I'd like to think it was something rather strange that gave you great pleasure. You always wear the same clothes. You never say a word. You never go anywhere. My son reads poetry and watches Hungarian films, what do you do?

BARRY. I play my records. And then I play them again.

JACK goes right. BARRY is alone. He looks at the top which is propped against the wall, then at the trestles. He adjusts them slightly, then goes to the top and tries to manhandle it towards the trestles. It's a two man job and he can't make it. He peers into the far workshop, looking for someone who might help, then determines to struggle on alone. He tries again, but can't shift it. GORDON comes back. He goes straight to BARRY. Wordlessly they lift the top face up onto the trestles.

GORDON. All right, Barry?

BARRY. I'm all right, Gordon.

GORDON. Good. Good.

GORDON goes off right. BARRY picks up a screwdriver and removes the first of the screws that hold the frame to the

*tabletop. He stops. Turns on the radio. We hear the Radio
Caroline jingle, then the Spencer Davis Group 'Keep on
Running.' BARRY returns to the table.*

Snap Blackout.

Scene Two

*One o'clock. BARRY has finished re-covering the table which
now lies face up on the trestles. He stands watching as CHAPEL
polishes the frame, dipping a one-inch brush into a jar of polish.
CHAPEL wears a good suit and scorns the use of overalls.
BARRY wants to go for lunch, but is unable to escape.*

CHAPEL. It's from the wrist, see. There's a knack to it. It's a light
touch. Light on the bristles, light on your feet. Move round the
table, don't dwell. You're working with wood. Work the polish
into the grain. Easy, easy. It's five minutes this job. You blokes,
you slap it on too thick. You know why you use too much?
Because you don't pay for the polish.

*TONY comes in with his case. He stops and watches. BARRY
surreptitiously begins to remove his workcoat.*

Full-size tables. That's how you learn to do this job. You polish
a full-size table, you know all about it. Thirty-seven feet of
frame in one easy motion. Up on the balls of your feet. Work
round the table. You wouldn't have the strength in your wrist
because you've never played billiards. Keep light and easy. I
could play the nursery cannon round and round the table, hour
after hour. Till they banned it.

BARRY makes a great play of looking at his watch.

BARRY. One o'clock.

He goes out, putting on his heavy overcoat.

CHAPEL. Where's he gone?

TONY. It's his lunch.

CHAPEL. I was trying to teach the boy something.

TONY. He knows how to do it. He's been working here for five
years. He knows how to polish a table.

CHAPEL. I'm not talking about polishing tables, I'm talking about
furniture. I'm talking about working *with* the wood, not *against*
the wood.

TONY. He knows.

CHAPEL. How old are you, boy?

TONY. Twenty-six.

CHAPEL. By the time I was your age I'd picked this business up off the floor and got it going. I expanded the premises. Where you're standing now didn't exist. I did it all on my own. My father was no good, you see. He started the caper off, but he had no vision. You put him in a room, he couldn't see beyond the four walls. In business terms he was an invalid. I had to go out into the world and make connections, then come back here, work with wood and cloth, sort out the botched jobs. I was up to my ankles in shavings till seven o'clock in the evening, then I'd go out and play a game of billiards with the nobs to draw in custom.

JACK comes in. He frowns.

I would go to Admiral Fisher's house in Queen Anne's Gate when he was First Lord of the Admiralty. Play the top brass, beat 'em, sell 'em a table. These slates used to adorn the homes of princes and diplomats. Now we stick them down some boozer in the Mile End Road. I'm not an elitist, but I've always believed in an elite. And now we don't have one. One man's sixpence is as good as the next. Well, not to me it isn't.

JACK. (*to* CHAPEL). There was a mix-up this morning.

CHAPEL. I wasn't in this morning. I had a business meeting.

JACK. About the van for the full-size. You ordered it for Monday morning. The table won't be ready till Monday afternoon.

CHAPEL. Why not?

JACK. Because it won't be.

CHAPEL. Well make 'em stay late tonight till they finish it.

JACK. You can't rush Gordon. He's a craftsman, he likes a good job.

CHAPEL. He's not been in. He's been collecting money from pubs. I've been working on the full-size with Arthur.

JACK. Well you should know then.

CHAPEL. I could start from scratch, now, alone. And have a full-size table ready for delivery on Monday morning.

JACK. That's not –

CHAPEL. Eight-thirty Monday morning.

JACK. You don't order vans. That's it. It's not your job to pick up the phone and order vans.

CHAPEL. You asked me to pull my weight when Len died. Well I did. You know my capabilities. I know wood and I know men. Put me in a room with a good saw and a good chisel and I can make a piece of furniture a Viscount would be proud to own. Put me in a drinking school anywhere in the world and I can shake hands on a bargain, walk out and sell at ten per cent profit. But I'm my own man and I'll do things my way. It's lunch-time. If I'm wanted, you can send a boy down the City Arms.

He makes for the door, right.

There is knowledge. And there is responsibility. And when you combine the two successfully you have power.

CHAPEL *goes*.

JACK. And when you don't you have a complete dog's breakfast.

TONY *smiles*. JACK *makes to go into his office*,

TONY. Don't go, Jack.

TONY *rolls a cigarette*. JACK *watches him*.

What's going to happen?

JACK. They want the Old Man out.

TONY. They?

JACK. Your father. Barry.

TONY (*surprise*). Barry? (*Pause.*) What do you think?

Pause.

He's got to go, Jack, you know he's got to go.

JACK. I know it's me who's got to tell him.

TONY. Why you?

JACK. Gordon huffs and puffs, but it's the eldest son who does the dirty work.

TONY. Tell him. That's business. But what happens then?

JACK. We muddle through.

TONY. What are we doing, Jack? Every day we re-cover two bar billiard tables, stick them in a pub, bring back two worn out bar billiard tables. Next day re-cover *them*, put them in, bring in two more –

JACK. A day's work.

TONY. A day's work. How many sites have we got?

JACK. Five hundred odd.

TONY. Five hundred and twenty-seven. And apart from the odd full-size, that's all we do, juggle the tables that are already there. We win some sites we lose some sites, but five hundred bar billiard tables is what we do.

JACK. It's a living. Compared with after the war –

TONY. After the war everyone was broke. We're in the middle of a boom. There's money out there, young money. We're just scraping by when we should be cashing in. This business isn't going anywhere, Jack, and businesses that aren't going anywhere are heading for trouble. Not now, maybe not even in three years' time. But in six years, ten years.

JACK. Ten years . . .

TONY. We have to do four things, Jack. I swear on my life this is the most important thing I've ever said to you. Four things. One we have to re-organise. Two we have to diversify. Three we have to expand. Four we have to set targets. That's your job, Jack, setting up the targets and making sure they get hit. That's a manager's job. That and asking the nasty questions.

JACK. What questions?

TONY. What happens when people stop playing bar billiards?

JACK. No sign of that –

TONY. No sign yet. What happens when it happens?

JACK. We think of something else.

TONY. Wrong. We think of that something else now. We get it ready. We put it on the market while bar billiards is still booming, then when the crash comes we're ahead.

JACK. Except nobody knows what the man in the pub will want to play in five years' time –

TONY. It's our business to know. This firm has had seventy odd years of experience. We should know.

JACK. We're a small business –

TONY. Because we think small. We could be a bigger business. Look at the space here. We could double, quadruple the turnover. All we would have to do –

JACK. We couldn't, Tony –

TONY. Why couldn't we?

JACK. Because what we do involves people collecting money.

TONY. So?

JACK. People we can trust. Which means family. And we're running out of family.

TONY. How do you know you can trust people in the family?

JACK. Well, they're in the family.

TONY. How do you know? I could be ripping the firm off every time I walk into a pub.

JACK. But you're not.

TONY. How do you know?

Pause.

JACK. You're not, are you?

TONY. No of course I'm not, but how do you know I'm not?

JACK. Because I know. I'm a good judge of character.

TONY. Well then. Use your judgement of character to employ honest people to collect the money.

JACK. We're talking about . . . how much are we talking about? Five hundred and thirty tables. Say fifteen quid a month each table. It's . . .

TONY. Ninety-five thousand a year.

JACK. Is it?

TONY. On those figures it is.

JACK. It's a lot of money.

TONY. The actual figure is one hundred and four thousand, eight hundred and twenty. I've been through the books.

JACK *is shocked.*

TONY. There. You can't trust me.

JACK. It's an awful lot of money.

TONY. Chicken feed. We could double it in a year. In three years we could be turning over a million. Now tell me why we aren't doing it.

JACK. We're –

TONY. I'll tell you why, because we don't want to do it. Look at this roof. It leaks in winter, in summer it's an oven. Look at your office. You spend your life there and there isn't a scrap of poxy carpet on the floor. We work in shit because we think we are shit. We don't want to make money because we don't think we deserve it. We're grateful just to make a crust. There's geezers out on the streets, Jack, they've got a tenth of your brains and they do half the work and they're running Rolls Royces because they think they deserve it. We're afraid of being rich. Because we're afraid it might make us happy.

JACK. We're a family, you can't change family.

TONY *goes to his bench, gets the brown paper bag and opens it. It's a draughtsman's drawing of a billiard table. He spreads it across* BARRY's *tabletop. It looks very professional.* JACK *studies the drawing.*

Did you draw this?

TONY. Yeah.

JACK. Very impressive. What is it?

TONY. You tell me.

JACK. A billiard table.

TONY. Nearly.

JACK. A pool table. American pool.

TONY. That's it. An orthographic projection of a pool table. With details of materials and unit costs.

JACK. The future.

TONY. It's mostly plastic to keep the weight down. Blue cloth to look different. This (*Points.*) retains the potted balls but keeps the cue ball coming back.

JACK. How did you do it?

TONY. I watched Paul Newman in *The Hustler* seven times and then I sat down and worked it out.

JACK. Seven times. Jackie Gleason was terrific in that.

TONY. Newman was good.

JACK. Newman was good, but Gleason was terrific. It won't work. Bar billiards, you can stick it in the corner of a pub, play off one side. Pool, you have to move all round the table. It would take up too much room.

TONY. So make the pubs bigger. Knock down the partitions. Make pubs like prairies. We build a couple of prototypes now. We work on them, stick them in good sites, refine them. We make more. We stockpile. Then we choose our moment. We go in and hit the market hard, before the opposition know what's happened. We take on more staff, we buy vans, develop this place. O.K. we lose small change to our collectors but we can afford it. Because we are smart, and we work hard and we aren't afraid of it.

JACK. Pool. What will the old man say?

TONY. The old man's finished, he's out.

JACK. You may be right. But just hold off. We've lost Len, we're losing the Old Man, we have to steady the ship–

TONY. I didn't have a migraine yesterday, Jack. I went for an interview. Shell Oil. Engineering section. You should have seen the place.

JACK. Did you get it?

TONY. There were six of us. And I was the one, no question. When they interviewed me, I hit every question off the middle of the bat. There we were, six of us in the waiting room – waiting room, there were plants, Jack, recessed lights, it was a palace and they use it for waiting – and the personnel officer comes in. I'm on my feet. But he calls another name. You know what he tells me later? 'Mr. Chapel, you're twenty-six years old and since leaving college you've worked in your family business making billiard tables. Do you realise how much less you're earning than all the other applicants?' And that was it. They picked a bloke who wasn't much more than a button pusher. But he looked better on paper because he came from Pilkingtons and took home twenty quid a week more than me. The place, Jack. It oozed class. And I didn't.

He suddenly kicks a cardboard box in the corner.

JACK. I'm sorry.

TONY. There are only two ways, Jack. You give me the chance to turn this firm around or I'm down the road and gone at the next opportunity. There's nothing else.

GORDON *storms on from left.*

GORDON. Clocks.

TONY. I'm sorry?

GORDON. Clocks.

The phone rings.

I said I needed two clocks for my rounds today. You said you would leave them on my bench. On my bench there are no clocks.

TONY. Shit.

GORDON. No clocks at all, is someone going to answer the telephone or are we no longer in business?

JACK goes out right.

TONY. I'm sorry, Dad, when do you want them?

GORDON. Half an hour ago.

TONY. I can get them.

GORDON. For half an hour ago, what are you, the Man from Uncle?

TONY. I'm sorry. I got behind with my migraine yesterday –

GORDON. I haven't felt well for the last six months –

TONY. Dad, we're all under strain –

GORDON. And some of us are buckling and some aren't.

TONY. Len died six months ago. We went straight into crisis. We all ran very fast in all directions. Great. Everyone reacts well to a crisis. Then the energy goes, and what are you left with. A way of working cobbled together in a crisis, that everybody resents but nobody questions –

GORDON. I just asked about a couple of clocks –

TONY. That's it. We look at the small problems, not the big ones. So when someone screws up, like me with the clocks, we blame personalities for the faults in the system.

GORDON. A family business is its personalities.

TONY. Well if it is, we've lost ours.

GORDON. What's that supposed to mean?

TONY. You know what it means. Do you want those clocks?

GORDON. What does it mean, 'We've lost ours.'

TONY. It means it used to feel good working here, we were a family, and now, thanks to you –

GORDON. 'Thanks to me', what does that mean –

TONY. It means 'Thanks to you', that's all –

GORDON. I'm trying to keep this firm from going under.

TONY. And I'm thanking you –

GORDON. I will not carry the can for everything that's going wrong –

TONY. Did I ask you to?

GORDON. I'm the one who's keeping us afloat –

TONY. You're the governor, right?

GORDON. I should be the governor –

TONY. You think you're the governor?

GORDON. Of course I'm the governor –

TONY. But you won't carry the can –

GORDON. If everyone let me get on with it and be the governor, nothing would go wrong!

Suddenly VICKY is there. The swing doors flap behind her. She wears a brightly coloured coat and a mini-skirt. She hesitates a moment, then turns to GORDON.

VICKY. Hello, are you Jack?

GORDON. I have a brother called Jack. Did you want to speak with him?

VICKY. Oh, then, you must be Gordon.

GORDON. My name is Gordon Chapel, do I know you at all?

VICKY. I'm Vicky Molyneux. You know my father, he does your accounts.

GORDON. Mr. Molyneux, yes.

VICKY. I'm working in the business now. My father doesn't have time to look through the books today so he's sent me instead.

GORDON. Did you receive a telephone call about this Tony?

TONY. No.

GORDON. Did Jack receive a telephone call?

TONY. I don't know, he didn't mention it –

GORDON. Well this is very strange, I don't know anything about any of this –

VICKY. I don't think Daddy called. It was very last minute.

GORDON. We have a long standing relationship with your family business. You've been going almost as long as we have. It's curious that we didn't know about this change in the arrangements.

VICKY. Well here I am.

GORDON. Tony, will you deal with this? Jack should be informed right away. I'm going for a bite at Mario's. I'll be off on my rounds at two on the dot and I want those clocks on my bench by one minute to two.

GORDON goes out, left.

VICKY. Is there something wrong with that man?

TONY. Yes, he's my father. (*Shaking hands.*) My name's Tony.

VICKY. Is it the end of the world that I'm here instead of Daddy, it's not exactly the biggest job on our books –

TONY. It is to us.

Pause.

He was upset. Before you came in. That's all.

VICKY. Why was he upset?

TONY. Because I made him upset. I'm very good at it.

VICKY. I have exactly the same effect on my father. This morning I suggested burning every scrap of paper in the office dated before 1956.

TONY. Radical stuff.

VICKY. But nothing doing, no bonfire. Not that I expected him to agree, I was just trying to get him going.

TONY. Why?

VICKY. Why did you try to upset *your* father?

TONY. Well, you know how it is. You wake up in the morning, something terrible happened to you the day before so you drank a little too much and the whole day after, and I'm talking about today now, you get on everyone's back.

VICKY. I'm having that day too. (*Pause.*) This place is . . . It's not how I imagined it.

TONY. You mean it's a pigsty.

VICKY. It's got history.

TONY. It's a pigsty.

VICKY. I mean in our office we have problems with the nineteen fifties, here things are a little more serious. Are you in this workshop all the time?

TONY. I get out a lot.

VICKY. I couldn't cope with this. At work I need good coffee, some plants and a window. You have to be up when you work in a city. A nice trip in a lift to a different world so you can look down. This would be a drag.

TONY. What would be more of a drag would be hauling two and a half hundredweight of slate up the stairs when the lift broke. We're ground floor people in my family, we open a door we expect to see a street. Do you have any brothers?

VICKY. No brothers, no sisters.

TONY. So the business will be all yours one day.

VICKY. It depends how much I want it. There's cousins and things, it's very complicated. What happened to you yesterday?

TONY. My pride took a hammering. How about you?

VICKY. The same. Now where do I find the books?

TONY. In the office. Jack runs the office, my uncle.

VICKY. Is he like your father?

TONY. He's more laid back.

VICKY. I'm glad someone is. What's this?

TONY. It's the slate of a bar billiard table. These holes at the end, they're easy but you don't get many points. These here are worth fifty, this one a hundred, but there's risks attached. This one here is worth two hundred, but if you knock over the skittle in front of it, you lose all the points you've scored in the game.

VICKY. I've played it. Some club off the King's Road.

TONY. Charlie Chan's. It's one of ours. I put it in there.

VICKY. I don't think it's worth messing around with those low numbers, it takes so long to get anywhere. And this is the coffee?

TONY. Yes.

VICKY. There's no such thing as instant coffee, you know, it's a contradiction in terms.

TONY. Well I won't offer you any.

RAY *enters left followed by* DAVID.

RAY (*jovially*). Where's Jack, I'll fucking murder him. We was well set up. The private buyer, you'll never guess who it was, oh hello, who are you, women aren't allowed in here.

VICKY. Why not?

RAY. Public health and safety. There's only one lavatory.

TONY. Vicky this is my cousin David. He's an intellectual, you'll like him. Vicky's doing the accounts. And this is Ray.

RAY. Pleased to meet you.

TONY. He's not family, you can ignore him.

RAY. You haven't guessed yet.

TONY. Ronnie Biggs.

RAY. Only Donovan wasn't it?

TONY. The private buyer? Donovan?

RAY. That's it, that Gippo with the big ears and the mouth organ round his neck. His birthday, wasn't it. His manager had him

out on the tiles all night. Brings him back, surprise present.
He's made up about it.

DAVID. He passed out on it.

RAY. Jack had set us up, he knew all along.

TONY. Did you get a drink off him?

RAY. Thought we was on for a fiver apiece. What did we get?
Flipping signed photograph.

   RAY *hands the photo to* VICKY.

VICKY. Nice smile.

TONY. Makes you weep.

RAY. Oh yeah, and David had a total mare. Got us lost with his
map reading, nearly dropped the table going into the pub, then
forgot to pick up Donovan's poxy cheque. Einstein isn't in it.

DAVID. Piss off.

RAY. I'll be glad when you go back to college. Now, a wet lunch,
a quick squint at the talent, then down the bookies to get on
Breasley. Where did your Dad go?

TONY. Mario's.

RAY. And the Old Man?

TONY. The City Arms.

RAY. Right, I'm going down the Blue Coat Boy. Anyone care to
join me, they can buy me a pint.

TONY. Take Vicky through will you? She needs directing to
Jack's office.

RAY. A pleasure. Follow me, madam.

VICKY (*to* TONY). Thanks.

   VICKY *and* RAY *go off right*.

RAY (*shouting*). Jack, you set us up something rotten!

   DAVID *takes off his work coat, goes to the sink and washes his
   hands*.

TONY. You didn't really forget the cheque?

DAVID. We had to go back. It was O.K.

TONY. Donovan.

DAVID. Want to go down the Blue Coat Boy with Ray?

TONY. I can't, I've got to do these clocks.

DAVID. She's a bit of class isn't she.

TONY. Yes, David, she is class, you're absolutely right.

DAVID *removes his work coat.* TONY *picks at a clock.*

TONY. David. You do another week here. Then finals. Then what?

DAVID. Well . . . I don't know.

TONY. You don't know. It'll happen in two months time.

DAVID. I just . . . I nearly enrolled on the teaching diploma course. Then I didn't.

TONY. Do you want to teach?

DAVID. No. I could do a postgrad course. If I get a good enough degree.

TONY. Doing what, studying a writer?

DAVID. I suppose.

TONY. Ernest Dowson?

DAVID. I don't think so.

TONY. When would that start?

DAVID. October. But I'm not sure I want to do it. I might take a year off.

TONY. A year off from what? You haven't done anything yet.

DAVID. You know, a year off. Decide what I'm going to do.

TONY. You're going to spend a whole year deciding what you're going to do.

DAVID. It's just an idea.

TONY. David, in that year, you could be doing something and finding out whether you wanted to do it or not.

DAVID. Like what?

TONY. Like working here.

DAVID. For a year? You're out of your mind.

TONY. It's in your blood.

DAVID. I can't do this job, Tony. I'm clever and all day long I'm made to feel like an idiot. That pub in Tottenham, no one there wanted to know about the influence of Horace on the verse epistles of Pope. I'm hopeless. If I were anybody else I'd be sacked.

TONY. You're unhappy here because you're in the wrong job.

You're working with your hands. You should be working with your brain.

DAVID. We move solid objects in and out of pubs. Where do the brains come in?

TONY. If you were in charge of advertising.

DAVID. Advertising?

TONY. The firm sets a target. We aim to double the number of sites inside an eighteen month period. We step up output. There's no pissing around. We employ more people to do the collecting. Your job is to persuade another five hundred people to put bar billiards tables in their pubs and clubs. How do you do it?

DAVID. I don't know.

TONY. I know you don't *know*, nobody *knows*. Guess. How would you do it?

DAVID. I'd . . . I'd go where the money is.

TONY. Good. Where is it?

DAVID. Young people. Upper class people.

TONY. The nobs, good. How would you do it?

DAVID. Well. Take Donovan. He's got a look, right? That's what we need, the right look, an image. It would have to be like . . . you see this rule chart, it sits over every table we take out. (*Holds one up.*) It should sell the game. But it doesn't. The player is middle-aged, working class and stupid. The drawing's wrong, it shouldn't be a drawing, it should be a photo. A young bloke, no a young girl with a bloke watching. It should look like an album cover, you know the last Stones album. It should say 'Rebel'. The name is wrong, skittle billiards, it should be something like . . . American Billiards. On the posh sites you start charging two shillings instead of sixpence so it feels classier. Then for the proles . . . you organise a tournament. Who is the best bar billiards player in London? That's it. Each pub enters one player. So there'd be a qualifying tournament and people practice for it so the table's being used all the time. You print a tournament chart, it goes up in all the pubs. The final, you book a ballroom, you get someone along . . . Joe Davis . . . pay him a fee to present the cup, you invite the newspapers, radio, television. You get people talking about it. That's how I'd do it.

Pause.

TONY. Now do you know what you want to do next year?

DAVID. It couldn't happen.

TONY. It could happen.

DAVID. Things are done in a certain way here –

TONY. Who decides how this company is run?

DAVID. Your Dad. My Dad.

TONY. Wrong. The shareholders decide.

DAVID. This isn't . . . Look, we're not having this conversation.

TONY. They're giving the Old Man the bullet today. If we make our move now, we can run this show how we want.

DAVID. I'm not in this, Tony. I can't do this stuff.

TONY. You just produced, at thirty seconds notice a brilliant plan for the next eighteen months, and you say you can't do it.

DAVID. I can do that, I just can't –

TONY. Yes?

DAVID. This is our father's business.

TONY. It's the family business. You and me are family. It's *our* business. If we don't step in, it's finished.

DAVID (*admiring*). Shit.

TONY. The A.G.M. is next Friday. We make our move. We lay it on the line. We say it's expand or die. We take my Dad off the road, put him back in the workshop where he's happy, full-size tables, a quality product. Barry becomes production manager in this workshop . . .

DAVID. Barry –

TONY. You give people responsibility they rise to the challenge. We bring in two new people to work under Barry, we make an office for you out the front where all the wasted space is. Inside eighteen months we guarantee to double turnover or everything goes back the way it was. Are you in or are you out?

DAVID. I . . . Can I think about it?

TONY. Yes, but not for a year. I have to know on Monday.

DAVID. I'm going for lunch. I need to think about this.

TONY. Think about it.

   DAVID *goes*. TONY *picks up a clock*. JACK *comes in*.

JACK. I know who you are. You're the man with the knife.

TONY. What?

JACK. When I was in the camp, it wasn't the Germans who were
the problem. Good crowd really, good discipline. It was the
other prisoners. Very rough crowd. Fight each other over who
had the biggest piece of bread. There was one knife in the
camp. Circulated for five years, the Germans never found it.
The owner of the knife changed continually. It was stolen,
fought for, used as currency. The thing to be aware of when
they handed out the food was who had the knife. You let him
have the biggest portion. The other prisoners always knew who
had the knife. But I never did.

TONY. Well this time you know. Are you going to give me my
chance?

JACK. I can't, Tony. Not yet.

JACK *goes.* BARRY *comes in. He carries an LP in a brown
paper bag and a copy of the Melody Maker.*

TONY. New record, Barry?

BARRY. Mmmm.

BARRY *hides the record away under his bench.* TONY *looks
at* BARRY. *He puts an arm on* BARRY'*s shoulder.*

TONY. Barry, I've been thinking.

Snap Blackout.

In the darkness, Donovan's 'Sunshine Superman.'

Scene Three

About four-thirty. An end of the week mood. BARRY *is working
on the base of a table, padding the channels with pieces of rubber
and occasionally testing them by dropping a red ball down the
channels into the ball-tray.* DAVID, *wearing rubber gloves, is
half-heartedly painting skittles.* RAY *is halfway into his motor-
bike leathers.* TONY *and* GORDON, *ready to go home, are
listening to* RAY.

RAY. So there's this old geezer, rich. Property, business, you
name it, and the doctors tell him he's got a month to live. And
he's got three sons.

GORDON. This isn't going to take long I hope –

RAY. Three sons. So he gathers them round –

TONY. Like you would –

RAY. Like you would yeah, three sons and he says, he says: 'I've decided to split my wealth among you according to how much you deserve it.'

GORDON. Quite right too.

RAY. And I'm giving you a test you to decide who gets most. So he gives each of them a duck.

TONY. A duck quack quack?

RAY. A live duck, quack quack. And he says, 'My sons, you have twenty-four hours to get the best possible business deal out of your duck and I shall divide my fortune according to your success.'

GORDON. Just think, if Jack were a bit sharper doing the wages we could have missed this.

RAY. Next day, same time, they're all gathered again round the old fart's bed. 'Tell me, my sons, how you fared in the world of business.' So the first son, right flash tosser goes: 'I took my duck to market and sold it for three pounds, which sum I put into your hand, oh mighty father.' 'Excellent my son', says the old geezer. 'You shall be rewarded.' Then the second son, bit fly like, says, 'I bartered my duck for a rabbit, then took the rabbit to market and sold it for four pounds.'

BARRY *becomes interested in the joke.*

'Excellent my son', says the father. 'You shall be rewarded even more.' Then the third son, he's not quite all there, he goes: 'Well father, I was walking down the road carrying this duck and there's this tom, says she'll do it if I hand over the bird.' So he follows her up to her place, hands it over, shags the arse off her. It's so good, right, she says to him, 'If you do that to me again, I'll let you have the duck back.' Fair dos, thinks the third son, so he stuffs her rotten again, she loves it, lets him have the duck back. Down the stairs he goes, out of her place, just crossing the road outside, when the duck flies out from under his arm, this Rolls Royce tonning along, slam, the duck's dead. Big rich geezer gets out of the car says, 'Sorry about your duck, here's a fiver for your trouble'. So –

CHAPEL *barges on from right. He's had several drinks. He points at* DAVID, BARRY *and* TONY.

CHAPEL. Boys. Old saying in the firm: a boy is a boy, two boys is half a boy, three boys is no boy at all.

GORDON. City Arms been open all this time?

RAY. Fuck's sake.

CHAPEL. Because if you hire one boy he does a day's work. Two boys'll skyve around a bit, do half a day. Three boys'll mess around so much they won't do bugger all. Like you three now.

TONY. We're off home, the week's over.

CHAPEL. You can't knock off just after lunch –

TONY. It may be just after your lunch –

GORDON. It is twenty-two minutes to five.

CHAPEL *consults his watch.*

CHAPEL. Twenty-one minutes to five. I must have been detained.

GORDON. By several large brandies–

RAY. You just shafted my punchline you old windbag.

CHAPEL. What's that?

RAY. I said did you see Scobie done my double for me?

CHAPEL. Breasley. He never did –

RAY. Three to one the two-thirty, seven to four the three-fifteen.

CHAPEL. Not much of a bet.

RAY. It's a fiver.

CHAPEL. Breasley. Not fit to ride in a public park. Not fit to hold Steve Donoghue's saddle.

RAY. More than I get paid for a day's work here.

CHAPEL. They talk about work, they don't know the meaning of the word.

RAY. Two tables a day, that's all I do on your wages.

CHAPEL. Work, a foreign country to the young men of today. You know what they say about family businesses. They're started off well by the first generation, consolidated by the second and ruined by the third.

GORDON. Right, I'm going, give the traffic jam a miss.

TONY. Dad, I won't be coming home tonight.

GORDON. What?

TONY. I'll come for Sunday lunch. And Saturday night probably.

GORDON. Your mother's expecting you for the whole weekend.

TONY. Well, it's just I've had a change of mind.

GORDON. This change of mind, I don't suppose it's got a skirt halfway up its bum has it?

TONY. I'm a free agent.

GORDON. I understand now. That's why your dirty washing got loaded into *my* car.

TONY. I've only just decided.

GORDON. An eat-while you wait laundromat, that's your family home. Your mother will be disappointed.

TONY. I'll be in Saturday night definite.

GORDON. And my name's Bugs Bunny. I'll see you Sunday lunchtime and that had better be definite, there's an H-bone of beef. Have a good weekend one and all.

GORDON goes left.

RAY. You don't half get him going Tony, got a sort lined up?

TONY. No.

RAY. Don't fib to me, you've got some crumpet promised.

TONY. Piss off.

JACK is in from right holding several brown wage packets. He wears a raincoat, ready for a quick getaway. CHAPEL looks at him for a moment, then fixes his attention on a box of old billiard balls.

JACK. Wages.

RAY. About time too.

JACK. Was that Gordon going?

RAY. Yeah. I'll be nicely stuck in the traffic now.

JACK. Thought you could weave in and out of it.

JACK hands him a wage packet.

RAY. I can't make it fly, Jack. Ta.

CHAPEL. They take money out of the firm. But do they ever put anything back in?

JACK (*to* RAY). You in Monday?

RAY. Tuesday, Jack. Tuesday, Thursday, Friday.

CHAPEL. Economy. Thrift. I've seen you young blokes sweeping new brass screws into the rubbish.

TONY. Give us the end of the joke, Ray.

RAY. Wait till I'm on Sunday Night at the London Palladium. You don't get interrupted there.

TONY (*pleasantly*). Tosser.

RAY gets his gauntlets on. CHAPEL has decided to find some viable sets of balls. He dumps the box onto BARRY's *table.*

CHAPEL. To the trained eye, everything is an asset. Give us that red ball you've got there, boy.

BARRY. I'm trying to work on this table.

CHAPEL. Give it here.

BARRY *reluctantly hands* CHAPEL *the ball, then flaps around, trying to find something to do.*

Must be a hundred odd balls in there, I lay you six to four we can find five perfectly good sets.

JACK. Wages, Tony.

TONY. Ta, Jack.

DAVID. Going to your proper job now, Ray?

RAY. No. Off tonight, aren't I? Got something tasty lined up. A shower, a shave and out. You can think of me at midnight, I'll be stuck up something rather dainty.

JACK. See you Tuesday.

RAY *is gone.* CHAPEL *rummages, looking for seven white balls of equal weight to the red.*

CHAPEL. We had a set of scales once to do this job. But I could always do it by hand.

He weighs white balls in his right hand, selecting and rejecting them. He throws the chosen balls noisily down the channels into the ball tray.

Three ounces, that's the specification. But I always went by the scruple. There, four already.

JACK *hands a wage packet to* DAVID.

JACK. David. The labourer is worthy of his hire. I'll see you later. You won't want any dinner kept?

DAVID. No, I'll get an Indian or something.

JACK. Only your mother's bound to ask.

DAVID. I'm O.K. See you Monday, Barry.

BARRY. Mmmmmm.

JACK. Enjoy the Hungarians.

DAVID *goes off right.*

CHAPEL. There. A set of balls. I'll put them under the polisher they'll look as good as new.

CHAPEL *exits left with the balls in his hands*.

TONY. You've got to do it.

JACK. What?

TONY. You said you'd give him the bullet today.

JACK. Well.

TONY. You can't cop out of this one.

JACK. Gordon wants it, Gordon can do it.

BARRY. Gordon won't be able to do it.

JACK *and* TONY *stare at* BARRY.

He makes all the noise. But when there's a dirty job, he sends in someone else.

TONY. Well this is fabulous. We've got a bloke who's taking home a wage for sabotaging the business and no one's got the nerve to sack him. Give me the gun, Jack, I'll give him the bullet.

VICKY *comes in right in her coat. She carries a brief case and some files*.

VICKY. Are you Barry?

BARRY. Yes.

VICKY. There was a message for you just now. Someone called Ian. He said it's on. You have to be at Eel Pie Island by eight o'clock.

BARRY *is energised as if someone has thrown a switch*.

BARRY. Are you sure? You should have let me speak to him.

VICKY. He was in a phone box. The pips were going.

TONY. What is this?

BARRY. Just some friends of mine.

JACK. Eel Pie Island.

BARRY. Some old school friends. They've got this group. There was a possibility that some support band would cancel. Probably, it seems to have happened.

TONY. And your mates have got the gig.

BARRY. Mmmm. Seems like.

TONY. So you're going all that way to watch.

BARRY. Well, yes. Is it O.K. if I make a phone call?

JACK. Go ahead.

BARRY *scuttles off right.*

Scenes of wild excitement.

TONY. All the way to Eel Pie Island for a crap R and B group.

JACK. Curious what stirs the human frame to action.

TONY. You said it.

VICKY. I'm going. I'll take these files away for the weekend.

JACK. What for?

VICKY. There are some things I can't quite work out.

JACK. Such as.

VICKY. Well. This fireman who works for you part-time . . .

TONY. Ray.

VICKY. Ray. There doesn't seem to be any record of his employment. Does he work here or doesn't he?

JACK. Well, he sort of works here and then again, he sort of doesn't.

VICKY. Well how many hours a week does he work?

JACK. Interesting question.

TONY. Depends how you define work really.

VICKY. Well presumably he clocks on.

TONY. They haven't invented that kind of clock.

JACK. Vicky. There's nothing to this job. You flick through the books for form's sake and then you tell me it's all O.K. Don't spoil your weekend.

JACK *goes left, brandishing* ARTHUR's *wage packet.*

TONY. He's right.

VICKY. It's my job, I want to do it properly. I've never worked on a family business. I'm learning, O.K? Now then, about tonight, where do we meet?

TONY. Walk down to the Angel, I'll pick you up. It's a black mini.

VICKY. Black mini, right.

TONY. Vicky. You wouldn't rather go out for a drink?

VICKY. We're going to a dinner party, that's the point.

TONY. It's just I don't normally –

VICKY. You're replacing somebody else at short notice. I've phoned your acceptance through. There is a formality in these things. Right now there is a sixth of a melon dusted with cinnamon sitting in a fridge in Muswell Hill with your name on it.

TONY. I won't know any of these people –

VICKY. At least they're not my relatives.

TONY. I can see the game you're playing. Vicky's brought a bit of rough.

VICKY. Better than Vicky's been shelved so she's come on her own. We had a deal half an hour ago. You're not going back on it.

CHAPEL *comes back with the renovated set of balls.*

CHAPEL. There. A new set, perfect. Five minutes work. Seventeen and sixpence saved. Vicky, I knew your grandfather. He was a gentleman and a scholar, Oxford man. But he knew nothing about life until he met me. I remember him as clear as yesterday, lying at my feet at four o'clock in the morning being sick into the Strand. Is he still alive?

VICKY. He died ten years ago.

CHAPEL. There you are. A good enough bloke in his way, but couldn't stay the course.

BARRY *comes on through the swing doors.*

BARRY. It's sorted out. I've got a lift.

CHAPEL. Where you going, boy?

BARRY. Eel Pie Island.

CHAPEL. Courted a girl on Eel Pie Island once. Walked all the way there and all the way back. I'd do it again.

JACK *comes back.*

JACK. You still here Barry?

BARRY. Ian's brother's picking me up here. He's got a Ford Zodiac.

TONY. Oh the flash sod.

VICKY. Well I'm going home. Some reading to do.

JACK. It's your choice.

VICKY. Nice to meet you all. I'll be in early next week.

JACK. See you then.

VICKY *is at the swing doors.*

And don't forget. The secret of accountancy is to ignore anything that looks remotely interesting.

VICKY *smiles, goes.*

TONY. Well. I must move too.

JACK. Nice girl.

TONY. All right. Give themselves airs don't they.

JACK. You tell me.

TONY *takes the rolled up drawing from his bench.*

TONY. I'll take this home, do some work on it.

CHAPEL. What's that, boy?

TONY. You wouldn't like it. It's the future and it's mostly plastic. (*Punching* BARRY'*s shoulder.*) Eel Pie Island.

TONY *looks* JACK *straight in the eyes.*

See you Jack.

JACK. I'll see you Tony.

TONY *goes, left.* JACK *hands* BARRY *his wage packet.*

JACK. Barry. Will you be able to lock up for me?

BARRY. Are you off?

JACK. Yes I'm going. Now.

BARRY. You're going now?

JACK. Yes. I'm off.

CHAPEL. No you're not. I want a word with you.

JACK. A word's not convenient just now.

CHAPEL (*to* BARRY). You. Make yourself scarce.

A moment. BARRY *thinks.*

BARRY. I'll put this through on the motorsaw.

BARRY *picks up a random piece of wood and goes, left.*

JACK. I don't want to have a word with you, Pop, I've got to meet a bloke –

CHAPEL. We've got to do something about Gordon.

JACK. Gordon? Gordon's fine.

CHAPEL. He's not fine. He's all wrong. One minute he's in the workshop, telling me how to make billiard tables, the next he's

tearing in and out of pubs, picking up boxloads of sixpences.
He's doing two jobs at once and making a pig's ear of both.

JACK. Well, my work's cut out in that office –

CHAPEL. My plan is this. I take over the running of that
workshop. Gordon does the collections and gone wrongs.
Specialisation. Back to basics.

JACK. Gordon'll never buy that. You're taking away the part of
the job he loves. Right back when he was a little boy he made
things out of wood.

CHAPEL. It's a sacrifice he'll have to make.

JACK. We'll talk about it on Monday.

CHAPEL. We won't talk about it on Monday. Come Monday the
phone'll be ringing. We'll talk about it now.

JACK. He won't buy it.

CHAPEL. Well what's your idea then? You're supposed to be the
clever one. Sit and think while the rest of the world is up and
doing. Tell me how I can save my business.

JACK. The business is fine –

CHAPEL. The business will go down unless, for once in your life,
you can come up with an idea.

JACK. What do you mean, for once in my life?

CHAPEL. Because the only one of you who was any use was Len.
Gordon, if you stand over him and hold his hand can just about
deliver. But you. I've tried every way with you –

JACK. You've never tried –

CHAPEL. I gave you every chance in life –

JACK. Not one thing. You never did one thing for me –

CHAPEL. – and you can't even come up with an idea.

JACK. Can't I?

CHAPEL. Even in the war, what were you? A prisoner!

Pause.

JACK. Well I have come up with an idea. Me and Gordon. We
don't want you to come in on Monday morning.

CHAPEL. If a bloke can't work with his hands, he can normally
work with his brains. But not you.

JACK. Or any other morning. It's over. We're finishing you.

CHAPEL. Are those my wages?

JACK. Did you hear what I just said?

CHAPEL *takes the wage packet.*

CHAPEL. I look around me now and you know what I see? I see people who think they're free. It's a form of enslavement, perhaps the ultimate form. Look at these boys working here. What do they want? They never ask themselves. They chase after things. But they never hold them, they never savour them.

JACK. Pop, I'm trying to tell you something –

CHAPEL. I'm trying to tell *you* something. When I was their age I was free. I came in here, fifteen years old, within a week I *was* a carpenter, six months a master carpenter. I knew the business. I could be a cutthroat, but I had the knack of acquiring a very difficult commodity. I had the knack of acquiring the love of men.

Pause.

Am I to understand you're giving me the bullet?

JACK. Face it, Pop, you're too old. The last six months you've done your stuff. Now we've got to look to the future.

CHAPEL. You're giving me the bullet?

JACK. We just think it's best if –

CHAPEL. Do it properly. Are you giving me the bullet?

JACK. It's the bullet.

CHAPEL. Well. I never thought you'd do it.

JACK. You'll get your wage as a pension.

CHAPEL. I always thought when it came, it would come from Gordon. I didn't think you had it in you.

JACK. When I came back. Five years in that camp, not a letter, not a parcel, you were eating a plate of kidneys. You looked up and said: 'We thought you were dead. You can come and work down the firm.'

CHAPEL. And it took you twenty years to stick the knife in me.

JACK. Well now it's done.

CHAPEL. It isn't done. I'm not taking it.

JACK. What do you mean you're not taking it?

CHAPEL. I'm not taking it.

JACK. It's the bullet. You have to take it.

CHAPEL. This is my business. I'm the largest shareholder.

JACK. Don't force this, Pop.

CHAPEL. I'll take it to a vote.

JACK. Don't take it to a vote.

CHAPEL. We'll put it to the Annual General –

JACK. Everyone agrees. Me, Gordon, Barry. Six hundred shares against your four hundred. Don't force it, Pop, go out with some dignity.

CHAPEL. I want to hear each one of you say it. You, Gordon, the boy. I want a motion and a vote. Then we'll see what you're made of. If you're giving me the bullet, it's got to come at the meeting.

CHAPEL *goes right. Some moments.* BARRY *comes back with the piece of wood, now sawn in half.*

BARRY. You gave him the bullet then.

JACK *stares straight ahead, rattling his keys.*

You did well.

JACK. You'll lock up?

BARRY. Yes, I'll lock up.

JACK *presses the bunch of keys into* BARRY*'s hand.*

JACK. I'll see you Monday.

BARRY. Monday, mmm.

JACK *goes, right.* BARRY *stands still. He hears the front door opening. He looks through the glass. He watches* JACK *go. Some moments. He puts the bunch of keys down on the table. He reaches in his pocket and pulls out a mouth organ. He taps it a few times on his left hand, then puts it to his lips and plays a sublime slow blues.*

Quick fade to blackout by the twelfth bar.

ACT TWO, Scene One

The Byrds 'Turn, Turn, Turn'. Lights come up on the workshop. It's the following Friday, just before two o'clock. Everything is the same except that TONY's drawing of the pool table is now pinned above his bench. GORDON and JACK, wearing suits, are killing time before the start of the meeting. RAY is completing last week's joke. Music fades out.

RAY. So the third son says: 'I got a fuck for the duck, a duck for the fuck, a fiver from the fucker who fucked the duck and I've still got the fucking duck.'

GORDON *and* JACK *laugh.*

GORDON. Oh dear, oh dear, oh dear.

JACK. Rather lost its biblical feel towards the end.

GORDON. I would gladly have waited another week.

RAY. Then there's this geezer, goes into a pet shop with a tortoise in his hand –

JACK. Please Ray, save one for after the meeting.

RAY. Suit yourself. Has the Old Man been in yet?

JACK. He was in for four minutes this morning. Gave a short lecture on the protestant work ethic then disappeared down the City Arms.

GORDON. We'll need a team of horses to drag him out.

JACK. Bought a new whistle for the occasion.

RAY. No.

JACK. Twenty-five guineas, New Bond Street.

GORDON. Well I hope he goes off quietly. Don't want any last minute nonsense.

JACK. He'll be fine. Been up and down all week but I think he knows it's the best thing.

RAY. He'll go out like a lamb.

GORDON. I hope those other earoles get here before him. We want that table ready on the nail for presentation straight after the meeting. Has Barry done the cushions?

RAY. I dunno. What we're gonna do, Gordon, is bring it through while you're in the meeting. Me and Tony'll do the final touches. You'll walk in, it'll be here.

GORDON. Well we're aiming at a short meeting, so if you've got the cushions to do, you'd better crack on.

RAY (*shouting*). Barry! If you haven't done those cushions I'm going to set fire to your Melody Maker.

He goes into the other workshop.

GORDON. Laurie Molyneux, where are you?

JACK. He'll be here.

GORDON. You did a good job, Jack, breaking the news to the Old Man last week. I hand it to you, I really do.

JACK. He cut up very rough.

GORDON. After I spoke to him Monday afternoon, he settled down a bit.

JACK. The time had come. The old clock on the wall.

GORDON. Comes to us all.

JACK. There's a thing, Gordon. Your boy, I'm wondering.

GORDON. Yes?

JACK. We want to hang onto him.

GORDON. Well yes.

JACK. I was thinking he ought to have a few shares in the company.

GORDON. Whose shares, Jack?

JACK. It's just, as it's happened, history, Barry has shares. I feel Tony should have some too.

GORDON. Whose shares would we give him?

JACK. Meetings like this, I think he feels left out. He's here doing a day to day job, he ought to have a crack at the overall policy –

GORDON. What policy?

JACK. Well, the A.G.M., we look at policy –

GORDON. We look at what, Jack?

JACK. How the year's gone, the prospects, the capital –

GORDON. It's a rubber stamp.

JACK. Well I know it's a rubber stamp –

GORDON. It's a rubber stamp –

JACK. It's a rubber stamp insofar as it goes –

GORDON. Jack, it's a rubber stamp. We look at two pieces of paper. On one of them is a pack of lies about the value of the site, on the other are a few numbers plucked out of thin air about the turnover. We sign the books with Molyneux and piss off home.

JACK. I know that, it's the principle –

GORDON. What's he said to you?

JACK. Barry has a voice, it's fair if Tony –

GORDON. What has Tony said?

JACK. I'm guessing. I'm guessing that's what he thinks.

GORDON. He's said nothing to me, Jack.

JACK. It would be a gesture if we gave him a few shares.

GORDON. Well, whose shares, *my* shares?

JACK. Not your shares, probably the Old Man's –

GORDON. We've just given him the bullet, we can't start –

JACK. I don't mean today, I'm talking longer term –

GORDON. Then David should have some. They split down the middle. If Tony got some of the Old Man's, my side of the family would have more than yours.

JACK. Just think about it, it's just an –

GORDON. If David wanted to come into the business, it would be unfair on him.

JACK. David's useless in the business –

GORDON. Well Tony's said nothing to me.

JACK. He's said nothing to me either.

GORDON. I'm his father, if he wants to say something, he can say it to me.

    VICKY *comes on right in her coat.*

VICKY. Afternoon.

GORDON. What are you doing here?

VICKY. I'm here for the meeting.

GORDON. Your father should be here for the meeting.

VICKY. Yes, he should be.

GORDON. Your father actually has to chair the meeting.

VICKY. Well I'm afraid I have a message from him. He can't make the meeting. He's asked me to chair it instead.

GORDON. You're going to chair the meeting?

VICKY. That's right.

GORDON. Why isn't your father coming?

VICKY. He asked me to tell you that a crisis has blown up at one of our big accounts.

GORDON. I see.

VICKY. It isn't true of course, he never had any intention of coming, our firm's got too big, he only used to chair the meeting out of friendship with Len. But he did ask me to lie to you so you would feel better.

JACK. O.K. End of discussion. Vicky will chair the meeting.

GORDON. That is impossible. That is not something that can happen.

RAY comes on left.

RAY. No sign of Barry. No sign of the cushions.

GORDON. What?

RAY. Unless he's stuffed them under the floorboards.

GORDON. He must have done them.

RAY. Well he hasn't.

GORDON. That table has to be ready within the hour.

BARRY comes in right flanked by TONY and DAVID. They've been to the pub. BARRY has his Friday record under his arm.

BARRY. What ho, Jack.

JACK. You three been on the booze?

GORDON. I thought you were doing the Old Man's cushions.

BARRY. Had a wet lunch instead.

GORDON. Jesus, Mary and Joseph. I swear none of this is happening to me.

GORDON storms out left. RAY follows.

TONY (*to* VICKY). What are you doing here?

JACK. Mr Molyneux is unable to attend. Vicky is chairing the meeting on behalf of the accountants.

TONY. What?

JACK. It's not your problem, Tony, you're not a shareholder. Vicky, come through to the office and I'll go over the agenda with you.

JACK goes off right.

VICKY (*to* TONY). I'm glad you're pleased to see me.

VICKY goes off right.

TONY. Shit!

DAVID. What's the matter?

TONY. Vicky is chairing the meeting.

DAVID. So. I thought you got on with her.

TONY. And you think because I 'get on' with her I want her around at a time like this. Shit!

BARRY is standing in the middle of the room in his overcoat, beaming. TONY walks over to the other workshop, looks in, then turns back. During the following, DAVID and TONY remove BARRY's overcoat.

Are you O.K. Barry?

BARRY. I'm fine.

TONY. You're going to be all right?

BARRY. I don't usually drink at lunchtime. In fact I don't usually drink at all.

DAVID. He's had too much.

TONY. He hasn't had too much, he's fine.

BARRY. I feel fine. I feel rather excellent.

TONY. Do you want to go through it one more time?

DAVID. Someone might hear.

BARRY. I know what to do.

TONY. Go through it one more time.

BARRY. Oh God, I go into the meeting, I get a seat as far away from Gordon as possible. Then as soon as the preliminaries are over I ask for a . . . what is it?

DAVID. Suspension of standing orders –

BARRY. Suspension of standing orders for a full discussion of the company's strategy.

TONY. They look puzzled –

BARRY. They look puzzled –

TONY. They fall off their *chairs* –

BARRY. I produce the figures. An estimate of the firm's performance over the next five years. I point out our organisational weaknesses and the edge our competitors already have over us in terms of plant, manpower and long-term planning. I suggest –

DAVID. You *demonstrate* –

BARRY. I demonstrate how our profits will fall year by year unless radical changes are made. They ask what's going on and I say I'd like Tony to be brought in to address the meeting.

DAVID. That's it.

TONY. He's going to be fine.

DAVID. He's going to be a sensation.

TONY. I walk into the meeting, guns blazing. There are three possible outcomes: one a complete cave-in there and then which we don't expect: two a proposal by Barry for an extraordinary meeting in one week's time with full participation by the whole family –

DAVID. What about Arthur and Ray?

TONY. – which is what we expect: three . . . things go badly. We're in the shit. The bullet, the knife whatever. And we say: 'Go on then, try to run this business without us.' Those are the options.

DAVID. Is this . . . ?

TONY. What?

DAVID. I mean . . . this is the best way of doing things.

TONY *goes to* BARRY *and puts an arm around him.*

TONY. This is the man. This is the man.

GORDON *and* RAY *come in from left.*

GORDON. Thank you, Barry, for not doing the cushions on the Old Man's presentation table –

BARRY. It's not a big deal, I'll do them now.

GORDON. You won't do them now – and it is a big deal – because a) you have a meeting to attend and b) Arthur did them and hid them in the slate room. He is now taking a very late lunch and expecting some kind of apology. Where's Jack?

TONY. The office.

GORDON. Only we need a word before the Old Man gets here. This is the end with Molyneux this is. We get a new firm on the job as of Monday.

RAY. Here Tony, did I tell you about this old geezer, goes into a pet shop, points to this tortoise, hands over half a crown and –

JACK *is back, followed by* VICKY.

JACK. I've gone over the ground with Vicky. We're just waiting for the Old Man.

GORDON. Good. The form is as follows. All shareholders, viz myself, Jack, and . . . er Barry, will be taking the Old Man through to the office for the meeting. Tony and Ray will finish off the presentation table. Alcoholic drinks will be available. David, here's some petty cash (*Pound note.*) for modest refreshments of the sausage roll variety. The meeting will be over within the hour. We present him the table, have a small farewell here and then whoever is still standing will load table, Old Man and any other personnel onto the van for delivery at Offord Road.

JACK. Pausing only at the Blue-Coat Boy, the Hen and Chickens, the Earl of Essex –

GORDON. Whatever you do, don't let him go through there and see the table before the meeting and don't get him going. We want no blood on the threshold, it's a celebration. Here he comes, look normal –

RAY. Pet Shop. Geezer. Tortoise. Half a dollar. Counter. Bloody hell, look at this –

CHAPEL *comes on right in his new suit, distinguished, relaxed. He is greeted by approving whistles.*

CHAPEL. Handsome is as handsome does. Not bad, twenty guineas.

RAY. Carnaby street was it?

CHAPEL. Carnaby street. When I was a young man, you couldn't give Carnaby Street away. You couldn't persuade rats to live there. Then a cartel of twopenny barrow boys move in and it becomes the last word in elegance. If that's progress then you're welcome to it.

GORDON. Well, you look very dapper, anyway.

CHAPEL. No one ever works in this place any more. People stand around in groups staring at one another.

JACK. We've been waiting for you.

CHAPEL. Well you can wait. I'm a gentleman of leisure now, at your request. I've been sixty years fetching and carrying, I think people can show me the courtesy of a few minutes grace at my final appointment. Is that accountant here, what's his name?

GORDON. Molyneux –

CHAPEL. Never liked the man. The sour fruit of noble loins. A proven cheat and swindler. That's why we've kept him on all these years.

JACK. Molyneux's not coming. Vicky's chairing the meeting.

CHAPEL. That's my point. The goodness in a family always skips a generation.

JACK. Well perhaps we should go through and get cracking.

CHAPEL. I was in a drinking school with your grandfather, the Grapes, up west. I said to him: 'Sir, you are a blackguard. Follow me into the night and we will slit the throats of some notable brigands at a game of draw poker in the Ball's Pond Road.'

GORDON *leads the way.* CHAPEL *and* JACK *follow.*

VICKY. And did you?

CHAPEL. We did. Jacks or better opens and we cleaned them out. We pissed champagne for a fortnight.

VICKY *turns at the door to address* TONY *but* TONY *is clocking* BARRY *dithering in the middle of the room.*

VICKY. Why haven't you phoned me?

TONY. I haven't had time to phone you.

VICKY. You had plenty of time for me last weekend.

TONY. There's a lot of things going on.

VICKY. Well tell me about them, then.

TONY. Go and chair the meeting, Victoria,

VICKY *goes.* BARRY *is rooted to the spot.*

TONY. Ray. We've got to move fast. Bring it through.

RAY. Yes sir three bags full. Come on David, if you've been wanking all lunch hour and haven't got the strength to lift it, I shall be most upset.

RAY *goes off left.* DAVID *makes to follow him.*

BARRY. I can't do it.

TONY *rushes to* BARRY *and shakes him.* DAVID *watches.*

TONY. You have to go in there and do it. When they send for me
I'll back you up, but it has to be you, right, don't, are you
listening to me, don't just sit there–

DAVID. Go on, Barry.

TONY. You will go in there and do it. You will not swallow what
they say. Change it, get in there and change it.

TONY *propels* BARRY *through the swing doors*.

Fuck! He won't do it.

DAVID. He'll do it.

TONY. He won't do it. Everyone in this family, talk, evade, never
do it.

DAVID. He'll do it.

TONY. Fuck!

RAY *comes back*.

RAY. Look I might be the tastiest thing in this firm, but I can't lug
half a ton on me jack.

DAVID. Sorry, Ray.

RAY. What's going on?

DAVID. Let's get it.

DAVID *goes off left*. RAY *looks at* TONY, *then follows*.
TONY *stares through the glass doors in the direction of the
office. He walks towards the doors. He presses his nose against
the glass*. RAY *and* DAVID *come back, carrying the base of a
quarter-size table. They put it down in the centre of the room*.

RAY. Thanks Tony. Any chance of a hand with the top?

TONY (*to no one*). Bastard!

RAY *and* DAVID *look at* TONY.

RAY. Tony, did you shag all your brains into that Vicky? You
haven't been yourself all week.

TONY. Sorry Ray.

DAVID. You what?

TONY *puts on a brown workcoat for the first time in the play.
Looking in the direction of the office, he backs towards the
other workshop,* RAY *follows him.* DAVID *stands gobsmacked
for a moment.* RAY *and* TONY *come back carrying the top.
They slot it onto the base.* RAY *and* DAVID *admire the table.*
TONY *looks out of the window towards Mario's cafe.*

RAY. They done him proud with this. Who was it?

DAVID. Arthur mostly. Gordon did a bit.

RAY. Tony?

TONY. Yeah?

RAY. Are you the gaffer here or what?

TONY. Mmmm.

RAY. Only, if this was a fire and we was waiting on your word, we'd all be well dead by now.

TONY. What d'you want?

RAY. Well, orders, leadership. It's like the war. They reckon the British infantry, best in the world but the officers are crap. Germans other way round. You put the British squaddies with the German officer corps, you've got yourself an army.

TONY. What are you talking about, Ray?

RAY. Don't mind me Tony, I turned into a tiny pile of cinders ten minutes ago. David, bolt that side.

RAY and DAVID start bolting the top to the bottom. The phone rings. No one makes a move to answer it.

Tony, answer that phone for fuck's sake.

TONY. Fuck off.

RAY. They're not taking calls in the meeting, that extension's switched off.

The phone rings several times more. DAVID goes to answer it. RAY stares at TONY.

Got a horse running in the two-thirty?

TONY (*turning round*). Right. Let's get going.

RAY. Yeah?

TONY. Let's get it bolted.

RAY. Let's get it bolted. Why didn't I think of that? I've got a good idea, let's use some big dollops of Plasticine instead, that should hold it together.

TONY. Stop taking the piss.

RAY. If there's piss there for the taking, I'll take it.

DAVID comes on. He carries an index card.

DAVID. It was the Sun in Splendour. The bar's not coming up. The clock's not tripping the bar when they put money in. So the balls aren't coming down.

TONY. And?

DAVID. So I said we'd send someone along.

TONY. Who did you have in mind?

DAVID. Well I said we'd try. It's the weekend coming. They'll want it working for the weekend.

TONY. Yes, I see that.

DAVID. The landlord's pissed off. Nothing but trouble.

RAY. What's the problem? (*Pause.*) What's the problem, Tony? I can do this. David'll get the sausage rolls in. Nip down the Marylebone Road, you'll be back before the meeting's over.

TONY. I know how to get to the Sun in Splendour, Ray.

RAY. Well, I can't do it, I'm not family, I might have it away with the coinbox and run off to Bermuda. And David doesn't know the insides of a bar billiard table from his own arsehole so it's down to you.

TONY. What's the number?

DAVID. What?

TONY. The pub's key number. Top right hand corner.

DAVID. (*reading index card*). Three six seven.

TONY *goes to a cabinet and picks a set of keys.*

Three six seven. (*Throws them at* DAVID.) Clock.

He takes a clock off BARRY's *bench, shoves it at* DAVID. *Does the same with his tool case.*

Tools. A to Z. Spirit level. Sixpences to try out the mechanism. Sorry, don't have a spare nappy. Unbolt the old clock, bolt on the new one. If the lever doesn't trip the bar, hit it with a hammer until it does. Don't phone in for help, no one will answer. These are the keys to my mini. Don't use them on the table, they won't work. And pick up the sausage rolls on the way back. Start here, start somewhere, this is real life. Now fuck off.

DAVID *stares at* TONY. *Then turns and goes out left. Some moments, then* TONY *turn towards* RAY, *benevolent.*

Now then, let's get this moving, it's the man's big day, we want it looking nice. Tell you what, Ray, take the balls through, two sets, billiards and snooker and buff them up on the polisher. I'll tackle this. Then the scoreboard, are we giving him a wall-mounted or a free standing?

GORDON *comes on.* RAY *stares at him.* TONY *has his back to* GORDON, *knows he's there but carries on.*

I reckon we take both on the van, mustn't forget the drill in case it's wall-mounted.

GORDON. Tony.

TONY (*turning*). Yes, Dad.

GORDON (*staring at him*). You're wanted in the meeting.

TONY *takes off his workcoat, folds it neatly. Goes to the sink, washes his hands.* GORDON *watches him. He dries his hands and turns towards* GORDON.

TONY. Are we going through?

GORDON. This is a *family business*.

TONY. Are we going through to the meeting?

GORDON. There is a code of behaviour.

TONY. I'm ready to go through to the meeting.

GORDON. Family. Business. Do you understand?

JACK *is at the swing doors.*

TONY. Are we having the meeting in here?

GORDON. I'm your father, you cunt.

JACK. Gordon. Calm it down.

GORDON. I am perfectly calm. I know what I'm saying.

RAY. Don't get involved, Tony.

TONY. Who's getting involved?

RAY. Just don't.

TONY. I'm just standing here.

GORDON. I know exactly what I'm saying.

JACK. Gordon, take it easy.

GORDON. I'm just waiting to hear some sort of explanation, that's all.

JACK *has produced a chair.*

JACK. Sit down, Gordon.

GORDON. I don't want to sit down.

JACK. Sit down, Gordon, don't argue.

GORDON *sits,* BARRY *comes in. He stands at the swing doors watching.*

TONY. Are we having the meeting in here or are we going through?

RAY. You go through, Tony.

TONY. There's no point me going through if everybody else is out here.

RAY. You go through, everyone else will follow in a minute.

TONY. All I'm interested in is the meeting.

RAY. Take him through, Jack.

JACK. Yes, Tony, you come through with me.

RAY. Go on, Tony.

JACK. Your father'll be through soon.

TONY. All I want to do is talk about the business.

 JACK *propels* TONY *out through the swing door.*

GORDON. Did you know this was going to happen Ray?

RAY. I just do the work and pick up my wages.

GORDON. Tony put you up to this, didn't he Barry? You haven't got the nous.

BARRY. I gave my opinion.

GORDON. And do you know my opinion? My opinion is this. I walked in through that door twenty years ago and someone saw me coming. They strapped this firm onto my back, and I've been carrying it round ever since, rain and shine, mostly pouring. And today we finally hold a meeting which is supposed to recognise me as the governor. And what happens? You (*Barry*) start complaining that it's not fair.

BARRY. I'm not saying that.

GORDON. You want fair, go and find another planet where they play billiards.

BARRY. All we want is a bit more efficiency.

GORDON. I'm not even talking to you. You're not the organ grinder, you're only the monkey.

RAY. Do you want a cup of tea, Gordon?

GORDON. We're meant to be in a meeting.

RAY. I'll make you a cup of tea.

GORDON. I don't want a cup of tea, I want to go back in.

RAY. Stay where you are. Don't rush into anything you might regret.

 RAY *puts the kettle on.* GORDON *looks at* BARRY.

GORDON. Do you know what your father said about you? The week before he died. He told me you were the biggest disappointment of his life. Not because you were ignorant and incompetent. He didn't mind that. What he minded was that you didn't realise it. So you could never get any better. Well he should have hung around a bit. He'd have realised the benefits of having a gormless son. He would never have got the hatchet in the back like I've had.

VICKY comes through.

VICKY. What's going on?

RAY. There's been a little quiver of excitement. Normal service will be resumed shortly.

VICKY. Gordon, are you coming through to the office?

RAY. He'll be back in a minute, darling. These long meetings, the modern executive needs plenty of breaks.

VICKY goes back through the swing doors.

Have we got a cover for that table in case the Old Man comes through? Are we still trying to hide it from him? Is anyone listening to me?

GORDON. I'm going back in.

RAY looks for a cover. GORDON stands. VICKY comes back with her coat.

VICKY (*putting coat on*). I'm off. I've had enough.

GORDON. You can't go. Whatever else we don't do, we have to agree the accounts.

TONY comes back, JACK is close behind him.

JACK. Come back, Tony.

TONY (*to GORDON*). You can't talk to me like that.

GORDON. I'll talk how I want.

RAY has found a cover. He spreads it over the table.

VICKY. You have two weeks before the accounts have to be filed at Company's House. I've left my report with you. I suggest you contact me if you have any enquiries.

JACK. You can't go.

VICKY. I'm not staying here if people are just going to abuse each other.

RAY. It's a fair point, Gordon.

JACK. Yes, let's get back in and talk it through.

GORDON. I just came in here to fetch Tony, I don't know why anyone else is here.

BARRY. Well I followed you. I just naturally assumed the meeting would be wherever you were.

CHAPEL *comes in. He stands at the door carrying a sheaf of papers.*

CHAPEL. All right. I want to say something. And I want you all to listen. There's been enough secrecy. Let's get it all out in the open.

GORDON. There's some people who aren't entitled to be here.

RAY. Give me my wages, I'll go home.

CHAPEL. Everyone will stay. Then there'll be no doubt what's happened. Open convenants openly arrived at.

GORDON. I'm not clear. Is this an A.G.M. or is it not?

CHAPEL. This is to be a discussion with votes. It can be ratified by the A.G.M. later. Right now, the priority is to get everything out on the table.

Pause.

There are three items to discuss. Firstly what the boy (*Barry*) brought up just now. Secondly my retirement. Thirdly the accountant's report. The first item is complicated. It's about how we run the firm. It's going to upset people. What I suggest is we discuss the matter after we've cleared up points two and three, but postpone any decisions to an Emergency Meeting next week. That would give time for consideration. Time to cool down. All right?

TONY. Fair enough.

CHAPEL. Good. So we'll get the other stuff out of the way. First my retirement –

GORDON. Just a moment, might I ask a question here? Will you be present at this proposed meeting next week?

CHAPEL. Yes.

GORDON. Then can I ask another question? If you're going to retire today, how come you're coming in next week to throw in your opinions?

CHAPEL. My retirement is the issue we're about to address.

GORDON. I'm sorry, but it's not an issue. It's something that's going to happen today, we've all agreed that.

CHAPEL. I made a verbal indication that I would retire today. But circumstances have changed.

JACK. You can't do this, Pop. We had this out last week.

CHAPEL. Why can't I do it?

JACK. Because we'll take it to a vote.

CHAPEL. Supposing I want to take it to a vote?

GORDON. Then there'll have to be a motion.

JACK. Well you've got one from me. 'This meeting requests the retirement of Mr John Chapel senior.'

GORDON. Seconded.

VICKY. That motion is now before the meeting.

GORDON. And I think we can move straight to a vote.

Pause.

VICKY. Well then. Shareholders only may vote. Those in favour.

GORDON *and* JACK *raise their hands.*

GORDON. Barry. Barry?

VICKY. Four hundred in favour. Those against.

CHAPEL *and* BARRY *raise their hands.*

Six hundred against. The motion is defeated.

GORDON. I heard it. From your own lips. You wanted him out.

BARRY. Circumstances have changed.

GORDON. I don't believe this.

CHAPEL. So we move to the accountant's report.

GORDON. I'm not accepting this.

CHAPEL. We need to get the books approved.

VICKY. The report. It's not here. I left it in the office.

CHAPEL *waves the sheaf of papers.*

CHAPEL. I brought it through. And I read it while you were all out here. It's very simple. It's what you'd expect. Except for one paragraph. 'In keeping with the practice of the past eight years, a bonus payment of one thousand pounds has been made to Mr. John Chapel junior and Mr. Gordon Chapel. In addition, this year the equivalent bonus that would normally have accrued to Mr. Len Chapel has been divided between his surviving brothers, so that each will receive fifteen hundred pounds.' The past eight years. Will someone speak about this?

TONY. A bonus? What is this, Vicky?

VICKY. It's hidden in the books. My father took a cut. I wasn't meant to find it.

GORDON. We pay ourselves a bonus because we run the firm.

TONY. A secret bonus?

GORDON. We do the work, we take a reward.

TONY. What work?

GORDON. Keeping this firm on its feet.

TONY. This firm is falling apart.

GORDON stands, goes over to TONY and throws a punch. TONY evades it and hits GORDON in the ribs. GORDON's knees buckle. He staggers back into his chair.

He hit me first.

GORDON. I'm all right. I'm going to be all right.

GORDON slumps in his chair. RAY rushes towards him.

RAY. Gordon. For fuck's sake!

Blackout.

The Rolling Stones: 'Paint it Black'

Scene Two

A couple of hours later. RAY is smoking. BARRY stands with his hands in his pockets. Both are looking at DAVID who is emptying a bag of sausage rolls onto a plate.

BARRY. So what happened with the gate?

DAVID. The gate wasn't properly shut. It must have blown against me.

BARRY. Blown? How could it have blown?

DAVID. The rain had just started. There must have been a gust.

BARRY. The gate couldn't have moved, it's fastened.

RAY. It moves if you kick it hard enough.

BARRY. We're talking about a gust.

RAY. And this was how long ago? David stop fucking around with those sausage rolls, no one's going to eat them.

DAVID. About an hour. It was about half four.

RAY. An hour, where've you been?

DAVID. I drove it off. I knew I'd done something to it, I thought I might be able to fix it.

BARRY. Where no one could see.

DAVID. Yes.

BARRY. But you couldn't.

DAVID. No, I couldn't.

RAY. Not much damage done, anyway.

BARRY. Severely scratched the paintwork, mangled the nearside handle and sliced all the rubber off the rear bumper.

RAY. New barrel for the handle and a touch up on the paintwork. Five quid, less.

BARRY. Complete new door panel. New handle. New rear bumper. Total respray of entire vehicle. Cost mmmmm, thirty-five pounds, forty pounds.

DAVID. Oh come on!

BARRY. Forty pounds at the very least.

DAVID. Well I can't afford that. That's what I've earned this vac. I've spent the last four weeks in this place for forty quid. Forty quid is what it's all been about.

BARRY. Well someone's going to have to pay, and it shouldn't be Tony. I suppose you want the firm to cough up.

TONY *comes on, left.*

DAVID. Sorry, Tony.

TONY. It doesn't matter. It's not too bad.

DAVID. How much will it cost?

TONY. Don't worry about it. It's a car, that's all it is.

DAVID. If you want me to pay –

TONY. I'll pay. Just don't mention it.

Pause.

RAY. What's going on in there, Tony?

TONY. He won't accept Vicky's accounts. And he won't go down the hospital. We keep going round in circles. You were right to walk out, Barry.

BARRY. I didn't walk out because we weren't getting anywhere, I walked out because I was being ignored.

TONY. Well, I'm buggered if I'm going back in.

RAY. Now I know why the Old Man was so chipper all last week. You lined him up, didn't you.

TONY. I'm not saying anything.

RAY. You promised to keep him on board as long as he supported you.

TONY. If that's what you want to think, you can go on thinking it.

RAY. You fly little tosser, I know you did.

DAVID. You hit Gordon, is that right?

TONY. He hit me first. I just reacted.

RAY. He went down like a pile of pennies. Honest, Tony, I thought we was gonna lose him. I was ready to give the mouth to mouth and he just pulled out of it.

TONY. It was a shove I gave him.

BARRY. It was not a shove, it was a punch.

TONY. I fended him off.

BARRY. If you want to get technical I'd call it a short-arm jab.

RAY. What it is, it's a warning for him. He wants to watch everything, his eating, his drinking, his smoking –

BARRY. Getting punched –

GORDON *pushes through the swing doors. He stands looking at* TONY.

GORDON. We don't seem to be able to reach agreement. Not on anything. Who runs the firm, whether I'm to be paid what's due to me, whether that old bastard is going to stop treading all over us, nothing. It's all up for grabs, apparently. So I've arrived at my own solution, gentlemen. I've just said my piece in there and I'll repeat it out here and I'll broadcast it tonight on the Home Service if necessary. I'm walking out. I'm going home. I shall be at home all over the weekend and I shall remain there on Monday morning. In fact I shall remain there until I receive a written undertaking that I run this firm and that you (*Tony*) are out on your ear. If you'd like to arrange a time with your mother when you can pick up your laundry, I shall make sure I'm out. In the meantime I shall expect a weekly wages cheque for doing sweet Fanny Adams. You have my telephone number.

RAY. Gordon, you've got to see a doctor. I swear it, your heart stopped dead for twenty seconds.

GORDON. Well. I shall now have the leisure to indulge in little hobbies like not running myself into the ground. I might even find the time for a migraine. Bastard weather. Good evening and the best of British luck to you all.

GORDON bustles out left. *RAY* follows him.

RAY. Gordon!

Some moments. TONY, BARRY *and* DAVID *stand around.*

DAVID. We should have done it differently.

TONY. I gave them the chance to do it differently.

BARRY. It isn't the money, it's the secrecy –

TONY. Asset stripping their own business. And we're working in shit!

He throws the open case of tools on the floor. The tools scatter.

DAVID. That's not the point. The point is, what happens now?

Pause.

BARRY. I don't see what the problem is.

TONY. I'm sorry?

BARRY. There's no problem. Gordon just said what we wanted to hear. It's him or you. That's what we wanted.

TONY. Are you nuts?

BARRY. He just said. He was going home. He was staying there till he was reinstated and you were kicked out. So he's saying, it's him or you. We, that is the shareholders, choose you.

TONY. The shareholders will choose me?

BARRY. They voted for you just now.

TONY. They voted for the Old Man.

BARRY. I'll vote for you.

DAVID. Gordon won't.

TONY. Jack won't either.

BARRY. But the Old Man will. They didn't cut the Old Man in on the bonuses, so he's not likely to vote for Gordon.

DAVID. He's right, Tony. It's yours for the taking.

Pause.

TONY. But this wasn't the plan. Screwing my Dad wasn't the plan. We're struggling, we can't kick him out. He's a craftsman. You give him a length of timber he can make it talk. And he's a businessman. The idea was to shake things up. It was going to be me *and* him not me *or* him.

BARRY. You can't possibly have thought that, Tony. He was never going to let you trample on him and then get up and shake your hand. We were gunning for him, that was the point.

TONY. We were not gunning for him.

BARRY. If you really thought that, then—

TONY. We were not gunning for my father.

Pause. DAVID *starts picking up the scattered tools.* RAY *comes back.*

RAY. David, you don't have to grovel every time I walk in, just mornings will do.

TONY. Has he gone?

RAY. He won't let me drive him home. I only stayed here this last hour to drive the fucker home. He won't even let me call him a taxi. 'It was just a dizzy turn.' I tells him, 'Look up dizzy turn in the medical dictionary, you won't find it.'

TONY. The stupid bastard.

RAY. Well it's *his* heart. If he wants to ignore his warning, he can die. It's not my problem, I never liked him.

BARRY. Tony, this is what we wanted. We all came into line behind you. If you back out now, I'll be left on my own, hanging on the wire. They'll just pick me off.

JACK *comes in, right. He sees* DAVID.

JACK. It went well, I hear, the Sun in Splendour.

DAVID. I fixed the table.

JACK. You fixed a bar billiard table and you smashed up a *car*. That's a net loss.

DAVID. The car is not smashed up.

JACK. It's a net loss. We can't send you out anywhere for anything. All you can do is sweep the floor and make the tea. We could get a woman in to do what you do. And he (*Tony*) thinks you could hold down a job as marketing manager.

TONY. Leave him alone, Jack.

Pause.

JACK. Well it has gone quiet. No one got anything to say? No bright ideas? Anyone feel like running this business, I don't, I never have. I didn't get the chance to go to University. Or own a mini. Or even a gramophone. What, no takers? There were an awful lot earlier on.

BARRY *puts his coat on.*

Off home, Barry? I'm sorry, am I upsetting you?

BARRY *collects his record from the shelf.*

A great contribution to the firm in your new role as a shareholder I must say.

BARRY *buttons his coat.*

RAY. Lucky you've got the coat, Barry, it's tonning down.

BARRY. I always have the coat, Ray.

RAY. Well I never noticed. Got your record?

BARRY. I'm fine thanks, Ray.

> JACK *tosses a wage packet onto* BARRY's *bench.* BARRY *puts it in his pocket.*

JACK. Eel Pie Island is it, tonight?

BARRY. It's a possibility. Good night. It's up to you, Tony. Let me know what you decide. You might see me on Monday. Then again.

> BARRY *makes for the door, his record under his arm.*

RAY. You've left your Melody Maker behind.

BARRY. You can have it, Ray, I've got another three copies here.

> *He produces a bunch of Melody Makers from his inside coat pocket. He waves them aloft and goes out through the swing door.* DAVID *is at the bench, looking at the open paper.*

TONY. Three copies, what's he got three copies for?

RAY. He must have been saving up.

> JACK *shouts at* BARRY *through the swing door.*

JACK. You'd better be in Monday.

> *But the bell has rung and* BARRY *has gone.*

DAVID. Here. (*Reads.*) 'On the Blue Beat with the Wailer. The dedicated band of ravers who turned up at Eel Pie Island last Friday were rewarded, not only by a fine set from Long John Baldry, but also by an interesting debut from North London combo The Storm for whom Barry Chapel blew a mean, sardonic harp.'

JACK. He blew a harp?

RAY. Mouth organ, Jack. Tommy Reilly.

TONY. He played. In public. Are you sure that's right?

DAVID. I can read.

RAY. Fuck me, he's probably a genius. Did anyone know Barry was a genius?

TONY. Eel Pie Island.

JACK. He'd better be in Monday morning.

RAY. Let's have a look at that.

RAY *takes the Melody Maker from* DAVID.

DAVID. I'm going to go.

JACK. I suppose you want your wages.

DAVID (*taking off his workcoat*). I gave it some thought. Working here. I was going to do it. I walked into the Sun in Splendour. The landlord said: 'I've had it up to here with your firm, skipper.' I said 'Leave it to me.' I unbolted the old clock, like you said, bolted on the new one. I didn't know what I was doing. The landlord was watching me all the time. I gave the bit of metal thingy a bash with the hammer, chucked in a sixpence, pulled the handle. And the balls came down. I said there you go, squire and he said, he said: 'They should have sent you round in the first place, will you have a drink?' I had a pint while a couple of blokes played on the table. Knocked it back, said goodbye to the landlord walked out of that pub, into the mini, stormed down the Marylebone Road, overtaking everything. I thought: 'I can do it, I can actually do it.' Coming into the drive, I'd made up my mind. I was going to work in the business, I was going to turn it around. Then the gate flapped and the whole side of the car scraped. And I knew I wasn't going to do it. I was never going to do it.

TONY. So. Back to your books.

DAVID. Yes.

TONY. Well. Enjoy finals.

JACK *hands him his wage packet with a glare.*

JACK. Where's your raincoat, you haven't got a raincoat.

DAVID. I'll make a dash for it. Oh.

DAVID *retrieves his book from the workcoat.*

TONY. The days of wine and roses.

DAVID. See you.

DAVID *goes right.* JACK *hands* RAY *his envelope.*

JACK. Wages, Ray.

RAY. Ta.

JACK. Not got your bike tonight?

RAY. I bring the car when I'm on the watch.

JACK. Well I hope it's quiet for you.

RAY. Friday night? Be fucking bedlam.

JACK. Thanks for what you did. I'm sorry about all the nonsense.

RAY. It's nothing.

> VICKY *comes on holding some papers. She stands by the swing doors.*

JACK. Don't . . . I mean, down the station tonight. Perhaps if you don't tell them what happened. Some of it, obviously. But not everything.

RAY. Why's that, Jack?

JACK. People might get the wrong idea.

RAY. I only work here for the anecdotes.

JACK. As a favour.

RAY. We see it all down the station, Jack. This, today, was nothing special. People are at each other all the time and we pick up the bits. A massive team of highly skilled technicians at your service twenty-four hours a day. Our number is 999. I'll see you Tuesday, everyone. Tuesday, Thursday, Friday.

> RAY *goes, left.* JACK *turns to* VICKY.

VICKY. I've just prepared a new statement. I've cut out all references to bonuses over the last eight years. Only this year's is mentioned.

JACK. The damage has been done.

VICKY. It's what Gordon's been arguing about.

JACK (*reading*). I'm not sure.

VICKY. I'm making it easy for you. Gordon might be away a long time, this'll be another problem you don't need.

> JACK *signs two copies.*

All right?

> JACK *looks at her, then goes right.*

TONY. If you'd told me . . .

VICKY. What?

TONY. If you'd told me about the bonuses I could have used it. Things would have turned out differently.

VICKY. And why didn't I tell you?

TONY. Search me. Business ethics?

VICKY. I didn't tell you because you'd stopped talking to me. I went through the books after you'd gone on Sunday morning. I came in specially on Monday to see you. You were talking to the Old Man and you glared at me. You flicked your hand at me as if you were brushing some dust off a cushion.

TONY. I was filling the Old Man in. I'd been waiting all day to get him on his own –

VICKY. Well, it felt great for me.

TONY. I had to explain the plan, it was the most important thing at that time –

VICKY. What was the most important thing on Saturday night?

TONY. That's not the point –

VICKY. What was the most important –

TONY. You were. O.K. You were.

VICKY. But I didn't last long.

TONY. I'm not saying that.

VICKY. I enjoyed watching you at that dinner party. How reluctant you were to tell those people what you did for a living. And then when the penny dropped, when you twigged that those solicitors and accountants thought it was cool. That they were delighted to shake the hand that collected the sixpences from the table in their local –

TONY. It was my way of coping.

VICKY. But the next night when I got you on my own, I thought, what I like about him is that he's straightforward. Which is why I wanted to tell you about the bonuses. Not so you might 'use it', but because I thought it would offend your honesty. Then you chose not to speak to me and kept choosing not to speak to me and I thought, what am I, a one night stand and he doesn't have the guts to shelve me.

TONY. I'm sorry. I couldn't cope with everything at once.

VICKY. What was I meant to think? One minute you were all over me, the next I didn't exist.

TONY. I'd still like to see you.

VICKY. No. I don't think that would be quite the thing.

TONY. I got distracted.

VICKY. For me, you see, it all has to hang together. You put things into separate boxes. I don't want to wake up one day in a separate box.

TONY. Just a drink.

VICKY. What for?

TONY. To talk.

VICKY. Not a drink. I wouldn't mind a talk.

TONY. Where then?

VICKY. Our office.

TONY. I don't want to see you in your office.

VICKY. I could show you the coffee.

TONY. I don't want to see you in your office.

VICKY (*handing him a business card*). I think that's exactly where you should see me.

TONY. Accountants and financial consultants. Bit of everything, then. (*Pause.*) I don't think so.

VICKY. Keep thinking.

VICKY *goes right.* TONY *stares.* CHAPEL *comes in. He's carrying a bottle of whisky.*

CHAPEL. That is a very capable young woman.

TONY. Yes.

CHAPEL. Distinction. You don't get that much these days.

TONY *is looking out of the window.* CHAPEL *is searching for glasses by the sink.*

TONY. There goes Mario. Six o'clock, the cafe's closed.

CHAPEL. Drop of scotch, boy?

TONY. All right.

CHAPEL *pours whiskies. They drink.*

CHAPEL. We did it then.

TONY. Yes we did it.

CHAPEL *looks at the quarter-size.*

CHAPEL. What's this table?

TONY. It's a quarter-size. Something my Dad was working on.

CHAPEL *pulls the cover off, inspects.*

CHAPEL. No money in these things. Who's it for?

TONY. I dunno. A bloke.

CHAPEL *opens the set of billiard balls by the table.*

CHAPEL. Today was the best business initiative this firm's seen
in a very long while. You said 'I want this, I'm going to get it.'

TONY. 'I want this, I'm going to get it.'

CHAPEL. You're like I was. A young man in the driving seat.
We've needed this for years.

TONY. Yes.

CHAPEL. I knew all that nonsense with the bonuses was going on.
But I ignored it. I waited to see if they would earn the right to
take that money home. And they never did.

TONY. What are we going to do?

CHAPEL *has placed the plain ball on the centre spot of the
dee. He takes a cue from the corner. He lines up the one ball
practice stroke. His stance is still perfect, his body assuming a
sudden gracefulness. He strikes the ball crisply. It travels over
all three spots, rebounds off the back cushion and retraces its
path back to the dee.* TONY *nods approvingly.*

CHAPEL. Plain ball striking. Did that half an hour a day for thirty
years. I'm going to take over Gordon's workshop. We'll have
to hire someone to do the collections.

TONY. Someone we can trust.

CHAPEL. You know the problem with family businesses. In a
family you have to protect the weak. In businesses you have to
get rid of them. In family businesses, the weak hang around
your neck like an albatross because you can't get rid of them.
So the strong get frustrated and move on somewhere else. What
happened today, we had to do it or you'd have moved on. It's
the trick I've been working here for the last fifty years, the one
I pulled on my own father. Shove the weaker brethren out of the
way and give power to the strong. And it worked.

TONY. My father's not weak.

CHAPEL. If he wasn't weak he'd have crushed you on the spot in
that meeting. But he didn't and you finished him.

TONY. I did?

CHAPEL. You did. How do you feel about it now?

TONY. Guilty.

CHAPEL. Be honest.

TONY. I feel guilty. (*Pause.*) I feel bigger.

CHAPEL. Good. Business is about getting to the top of the heap. My sons have always made a mistake. They think business is about getting by. They don't have that urge to put one over on the other bloke. You've got that. Want another?

TONY. No thanks.

CHAPEL *pours himself another drink,* JACK *comes back,*

CHAPEL. It's not a bad table. Cushions a bit sloppy.

CHAPEL *browses in the sausage rolls.*

JACK. Are you going home, Pop? It's throwing it down.

CHAPEL. I've seen worse weather. These sausage rolls are all right, where did he get them?

TONY. Mario's.

CHAPEL. Done well that Italian boy. Now then. I'll just take a butcher's at the order book.

CHAPEL *tosses back the drink and strides into the other workshop.*

JACK. You know, I always envied Gordon because he had you. I wanted you for my son the way some men want other men's wives. I hate this place. It's a nowhere job. It's been a nowhere job for twenty years. But when you walked in that door for your first day's work, I thought, this is it, at last we're going somewhere.

TONY. I used to like coming here when I was a boy. Saturday morning treat. Run up the road, open the front door, the bell would ring and I would hear you banging out an invoice or something on the typewriter. And when I pushed open the door you'd turn and smile.

JACK *goes to the window. He stares out at the rain.*

I had to do it today, Jack. You left me no choice. I offered you the easy way and you wouldn't take it.

JACK. I would have taken it. We just needed more time.

TONY. How much more time?

JACK. Just enough to get sorted out.

TONY. How much time is that? (*Points off.*) That man out there is seventy-five years old and he's still giving you your orders.

JACK. I fired him last week.

TONY. Twenty years late.

JACK. I still fired him. Not Gordon, me. I gave him the bullet, right between the eyes. And today you brought him back.

TONY. Because he was the one man in this firm who listened to me. He knew I was the future and he had the nous to put his money on me.

JACK. He used you. He doesn't care about the firm. He only cares about himself.

Pause.

TONY. Fucking rain.

JACK. What are we going to do? Your father says he won't work with you.

TONY. That's right.

JACK. But we need both of you. We're stretched as it is.

TONY. I know.

JACK. We could play it like this. We make Gordon take a couple of weeks off. His health. A month. We ease him back in, three days a week while you're on holiday. You come back. There's water under the bridge. Forgive and forget. The routine takes over. Slowly we get back to normal.

TONY. No, Jack. There's no more slowly.

JACK. So you're saying . . . you're saying we pension him off. It would cost too much, we'd be paying Gordon a manager's salary for pottering round his garden . . .

TONY. Plus bonuses.

JACK. Is that what you're saying?

TONY *goes to his bench. He takes down the drawing of the pool table and rolls it up.*

TONY. I told you last week. This is the future.

JACK. What are you saying?

TONY. It's me or my Dad. That's fine. It's his business. He can stay.

JACK. You can't go.

TONY *begins to pack his tool case.*

We can't cope without you. It's not physically possible.

TONY. Then hire some people.

JACK. We can't hire some people, we've been through this, it's a question of trust.

TONY. You don't trust me. And I don't trust you. It's not a problem any more. Phone up the labour exchange, bring in some blokes. If they rob you, fire them. Or don't fire them. It doesn't matter.

JACK. But if you go . . . David's no good. Barry will drift off. We'll keep going for ten years. And then the business will close. It'll all end in nothing.

TONY. That's right.

JACK. And what will you do?

TONY (*brandishes plan*). This.

JACK. Pool tables.

TONY. Pool tables.

JACK. On your own? It's not possible.

TONY. Anything's possible.

JACK. You've got nothing. You need premises. Tools.

TONY. I know what I know.

JACK. That's not enough.

TONY. I know what I know. I just need capital.

JACK. Where are you going to get capital?

TONY. I've set up a meeting.

JACK. What meeting?

TONY. Someone I know.

JACK. You've got finance.

TONY. I might have finance. It's in the pipeline.

JACK. You had all this prepared?

TONY. Nope.

JACK. But you reckon you can go it alone.

TONY *is ready to go.*

You can change your mind.

TONY. Yeah, I know.

JACK. You can always change your mind.

TONY. Jack. I'm sorry if I disappointed you.

JACK. It's O.K.

TONY. No, I really am sorry.

JACK. It's O.K. Tony.

TONY *goes.* JACK *stands for a moment.* CHAPEL *comes on from left with a piece of paper.*

CHAPEL. He's supposed to be starting a full-size on Monday for Clerkenwell Boy's Club. Needs to be ready Friday afternoon.

JACK. Well.

CHAPEL. That girl'll go far, mark my words. She'll pick their firm off the floor when her father pops off.

JACK. Yes.

CHAPEL. It's not such a bad thing, what happened today. You've got to give the young boys their head.

Pause.

You want to come for a quick one down the City Arms?

JACK. No, Pop, I'm off home.

CHAPEL. Well. I'll be having one.

JACK. It's raining hard.

CHAPEL. I'll get a cab from the pub.

JACK. Suit yourself.

CHAPEL. That full-size. I'll be in Monday morning.

CHAPEL *goes right.* JACK *stands by the table. Runs his fingers along the nap of the cloth. He gets the bunch of keys out of his pocket. He shakes them a little. Then stops, looks at them. He shakes them with sudden force until they make a ringing sound. He stops. He stares ahead.*

Music fades in – the harmonica break from Sonny Boy Williamson's 'Trust my Baby'. Slow fade to

Blackout.